# Accountability

*Managing for Maximum Results*

**Sam R. Lloyd**

***A Fifty-Minute™ Series Book***

This Fifty-Minute™ book is designed to be "read with a pencil." It is an excellent workbook for self-study as well as classroom learning. All material is copyright-protected and cannot be duplicated without permission from the publisher. *Therefore, be sure to order a copy for every training participant by contacting:*

**1-800-442-7477**

**CrispLearning.com**

# Accountability

*Managing for Maximum Results*

**Sam R. Lloyd**

**CREDITS:**
Senior Editor: **Debbie Woodbury**
Editor: **Ann Gosch**
Assistant Editor: **Genevieve Del Rosario**
Production Manager: **Judy Petry**
Design: **Nicole Phillips**
Production Artist: **Zach Hooker**
Cartoonist: **Ralph Mapson**


Printed in the United States of America by Von Hoffmann Graphics, Inc.

**CrispLearning.com**

01 02 03 04 10 9 8 7 6 5 4 3 2 1

Library of Congress Catalog Card Number 2001095523
Lloyd, Sam R.
Accountability
ISBN 1-56052-647-5

# Learning Objectives For:

## ACCOUNTABILITY

The objectives for *Accountability* are listed below. They have been developed to guide you, the reader, to the core issues covered in this book.

### THE OBJECTIVES OF THIS BOOK ARE:

❑ 1) To explain how building relationships that support maximum accountability is beneficial to the organization and the individual.

❑ 2) To describe how to establish positive expectations and rapport through the use of active listening skills.

❑ 3) To explain how to delegate effectively so that employees are empowered and motivated to be accountable for results.

❑ 4) To provide tips and tools for improving communications and creating win-win relationships.

### ASSESSING YOUR PROGRESS

In addition to the learning objectives, Crisp Learning has developed an **assessment** that covers the fundamental information presented in this book. A 25-item, multiple-choice and true-false questionnaire allows the reader to evaluate his or her comprehension of the subject matter. To learn how to obtain a copy of this assessment, please call **1-800-442-7477** and ask to speak with a Customer Service Representative.

*Assessments should not be used in any employee selection process.*

# About the Author

Sam R. Lloyd is President of SuccessSystems, Inc., an international training and consulting firm based in Boulder, Colorado. Sam has worked with organizations for over 25 years providing training for a wide variety of individual and organizational needs. Sam served for 10 years as a university faculty member and administrator, and has a background in sales, sales training and supervision in the insurance industry. Besides heading SuccessSystems for 20 years, Sam has also completed all coursework for his Ph.D. in Organizational Behavior. In addition to *Accountability*, Sam is the author of *Developing Positive Assertiveness*, and co-author of *Self-Empowerment*, both by Crisp Publications.

Sam designed, developed, and directed hundreds of seminars and short courses for the business community during his years as Assistant Dean of the School of Business Administration at the University of Missouri-St. Louis, and as Director of the Management Center at Southern Methodist University in Dallas. He has been an active member and leader of several associations including the International and USA Transactional Analysis Associations, the Administrative Management Society, the American Society for Training and Development and the Society for Human Resource Management.

## *How to Use This Book*

This *Fifty-Minute*™ *Series Book* is a unique, user-friendly product. As you read through the material, you will quickly experience the interactive nature of the book. There are numerous exercises, real-world case studies, and examples that invite your opinion, as well as checklists, tips, and concise summaries that reinforce your understanding of the concepts presented.

A Crisp Learning *Fifty-Minute*™ *Book* can be used in variety of ways. Individual self-study is one of the most common. However, many organizations use *Fifty-Minute* books for pre-study before a classroom training session. Other organizations use the books as a part of a system-wide learning program–supported by video and other media based on the content in the books. Still others work with Crisp Learning to customize the material to meet their specific needs and reflect their culture. Regardless of how it is used, we hope you will join the more than 20 million satisfied learners worldwide who have completed a *Fifty-Minute Book.*

# Preface

For any organization to be consistently successful, the people who work there must perform at high levels; must communicate often and well; and must be innovative, well trained, and talented. They must be able to depend upon one another to keep their commitments, perform their jobs, and be honest about how things are going.

Accepting these responsibilities and the consequences that may result from them are what accountability is all about. Accountability also means being able to demonstrate and possibly document the results achieved. When everyone is accountable, then all can work together with a much higher level of trust and cooperation and achieve real teamwork.

In this book you will learn about the components of accountability, particularly how to manage others to improve their ability and willingness to be accountable. You can't just demand it. You can't just have a policy requiring it. You can't just ask people to be more accountable. To develop accountability, you have to encourage, nurture, teach, and reward it in others. My other book, *Self-Empowerment,* co-authored by Tina Berthelot, is full of tips and techniques to help individuals discover their own path to becoming more empowered and accountable.

If you implement the ideas in this book and develop the skills presented, you will increase the accountability competence in those you supervise. They will benefit by performing at higher levels of excellence, and you will have employees whom you can count on. That is a win-win outcome.

I wish you success in using these ideas and techniques!

Sam R. Lloyd

Sam R. Lloyd

SuccessSystems, Inc.

Boulder, Colorado

# Contents

## Part 4: Communication Tools That Build Accountability



## Part 5: Follow-up Ideas for Skill Development



## Appendix

# PART 1

# The Case for Accountability

# Getting Work Done Through Others

Those who work with organizations and managers to identify competencies needed at various organizational levels have discovered that accountability comes up repeatedly. Whether at the executive or entry level, employees must agree to be accountable for the choices they make and the outcomes that result.

Why be concerned about accountability? A basic reason stems from the very definition of a manager.

**Manager** (ma'•ni•jər), n. - Someone who gets work done through others

Sounds simple enough, right? Hardly. Many skills are required to get work done through others. When these skills are used well, the benefits are substantial.

| Managerial Skill | How It Fosters Accountability |
|---|---|
| Goal setting and contracting for results | Clearly defines expectations |
| Delegation | Empowers employees |
| Monitoring without "looking over shoulder" | Communicates trust |
| Facilitating solutions | Develops employee's abilities |
| Coaching/correcting | Improves performance/confidence |
| Recognition and rewards | Reinforces desired behavior |
| Respectful communication | Strengthens relationships |

Ideas and techniques for developing these managerial skills are provided in this book. The manager must be able to depend upon employees accepting responsibility for tasks and results. Without this accountability, the manager will experience a great deal of uncertainty about how well things are being done.

Employees also will have a stronger investment in the assignment when they know they are responsible for the results and are trusted to use their judgment in obtaining the results. This is sometimes referred to as "ownership." Does this really make a difference?

Think about this for a minute: Have you ever driven a rental car? If so, did you wash it before you returned it? Probably not. People who *own* cars are more inclined to wash them regularly. If you have owned rental property, you may have discovered that renters often take little responsibility for caring for the property. Ownership, whether in things or ideas, promotes accountability.

## Case Study: Sharing the Workload

Kelly, a manager, was working 60 hours a week and falling farther and farther behind each week. She realized it was time to delegate some work and selected Bob for an assignment. Knowing that Bob was also working long hours, Kelly was a little uncomfortable giving him more to do but knew it was necessary.

The delegation discussion went something like this: "Hey, Bob, I hate to have to do this, but I have to ask you to take some work off my hands so I can get the production report finished before the quarterly meeting. I'm way behind and my boss will have my head if I don't have that report ready! Would you mind going through these reports from the quality task force and giving me a summary?"

Bob avoided eye contact and mumbled, "I'm not sure when I'll have time for it, but I guess I could at least look them over for you."

Kelly responded with relief, "Great, great! I knew I could count on you, Bob."

A few weeks later when Kelly asked Bob for the reports and his summary, Bob said he had not yet had time to go through them. Kelly exploded. "What do you mean you haven't had time? You knew I was counting on you to evaluate those recommendations so I could make my decisions on them without having to spend hours reading all that data! I have to have my report ready by Wednesday's executive meeting and you haven't done a lick of work!"

What a mess! The employee failed to carry out Kelly's wishes and the relationship was damaged.

What went wrong? Check (✔) the answers below that you think best identify the problems in this case.

❑ 1. The employee resented being given extra work.

❑ 2. The manager did not establish deadlines.

❑ 3. The delegation communication was tentative, nonassertive.

❑ 4. The employee did not ask for clarification about the assignment.

❑ 5. The manager did not stress the importance and priority of the assignment.

*Compare your responses to the author's suggestions in the Appendix.*

## Evaluate Your Skills

To get a quick reading on how you have been managing your relationships with employees and others, rank yourself using the following scale. Be honest to get the most accurate reading.

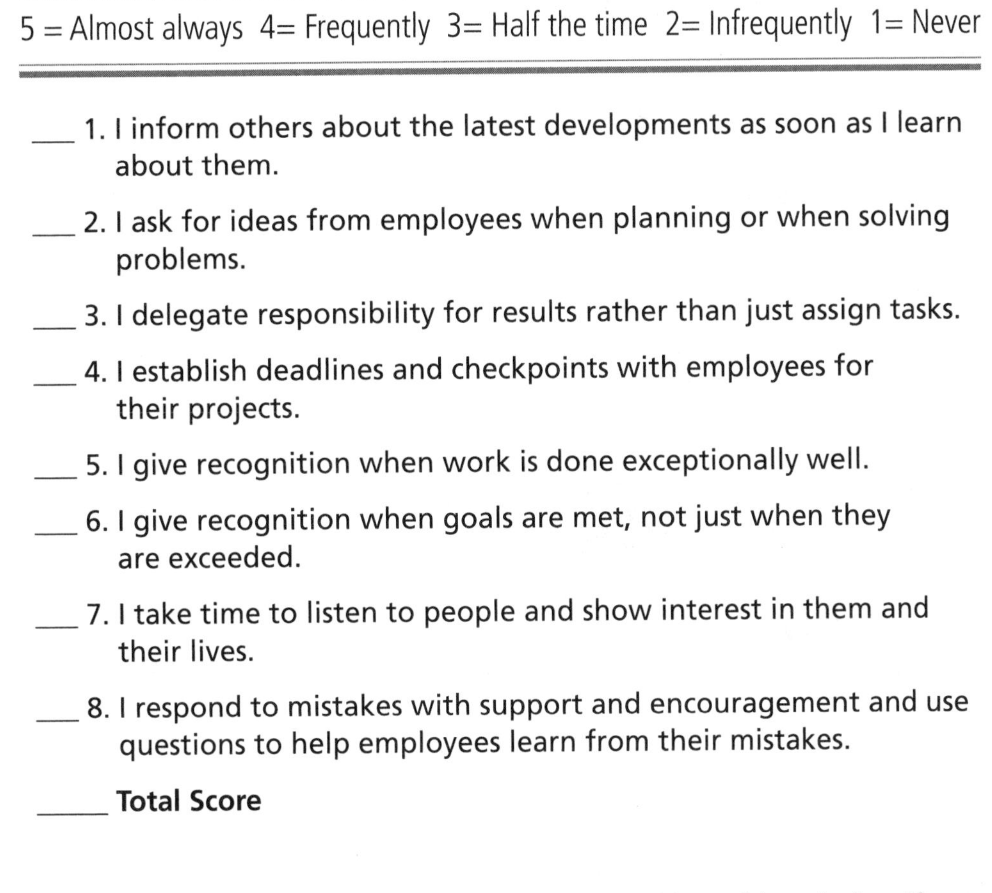

5 = Almost always 4= Frequently 3= Half the time 2= Infrequently 1= Never

___ 1. I inform others about the latest developments as soon as I learn about them.

___ 2. I ask for ideas from employees when planning or when solving problems.

___ 3. I delegate responsibility for results rather than just assign tasks.

___ 4. I establish deadlines and checkpoints with employees for their projects.

___ 5. I give recognition when work is done exceptionally well.

___ 6. I give recognition when goals are met, not just when they are exceeded.

___ 7. I take time to listen to people and show interest in them and their lives.

___ 8. I respond to mistakes with support and encouragement and use questions to help employees learn from their mistakes.

_____ **Total Score**

How did you do? The ideal manager would score 40 on this quiz, but if you scored in the 20s, you are among the better managers. Those items on which you scored a 3 or below are indicators of where you could improve in managing your relationships to develop better accountability in others. You will gain many more ideas as you continue.

# Gathering Feedback

As you probably know, you are not always the best judge of your own behavior. To discover how others perceive you and your managerial behavior, you may reproduce the questionnaire on the next page–a variation of the quiz you just completed–and give it to your employees and peers. This may take a little courage on your part, but doing so will give you more knowledge about where to concentrate your improvement efforts as you continue to work through this book.

To help your employees feel comfortable, you may distribute the questionnaires in a meeting. This way they will see that everyone receives a form and that the forms are not coded to identify who has completed them. They will see that they do not have to sign the form. If they just check the items, their handwriting will not even appear on the form.

# How Am I Doing?

I would like to improve as a manager, and you can help by completing this brief questionnaire. Your honest answers will help me identify areas for improvement. To help you feel comfortable giving me honest feedback, you may remain anonymous. If you choose to complete the open-ended question, you can print your response and attach it to the quiz. Thank you for your help!

5 = Almost always 4= Frequently 3= Half the time 2= Infrequently 1= Never

_____ 1. I inform others about the latest developments as soon as I learn about them.

_____ 2. I ask for ideas from employees when planning or when solving problems.

_____ 3. I delegate responsibility for results rather than just assign tasks.

_____ 4. I establish deadlines and checkpoints with employees for their projects.

_____ 5. I give recognition when work is done exceptionally well.

_____ 6. I give recognition when goals are met as well as when they are exceeded.

_____ 7. I take time to listen to people and show interest in them and their lives.

_____ 8. I respond to mistakes with support and encouragement and use questions to help employees learn from their mistakes.

What do you think I could do more effectively?

_______________________________________________

_______________________________________________

_______________________________________________

_______________________________________________

_______________________________________________

*P A R T* **2**

# The Manager/ Employee Relationship

# Establishing Positive Expectations

In Part 1 you read that the relationship between manager and employee is the key to maximum accountability. A relationship built on mutual trust and respect, effective communication, and good problem-solving skills is more likely to foster accountability for achieving desired results.

## *Self-Fulfilling Prophecy*

A manager can encourage desired results from employees or might set the stage for failure, depending on the use of self-fulfilling prophecy. When this powerful dynamic takes place between two people, it works something like this: Day after day, one person sends to another person subtle messages that communicate expectations. Often these messages are unintentional and below conscious awareness, but they do tell the other person what is expected of him. The message may be communicated with signals as subtle as a raised eyebrow, a head shake, a facial expression, a voice tone. The result is that the receiver of the messages usually behaves just the way the sender expected him to.

### Case Study: A Negative Self-Fulfilling Prophecy

Wednesday: Casey, the manager, is listening as Pat, the employee, explains an idea for improving customer service. Pat notices several times during the explanation that Casey's head is subtly shaking from side to side.

Thursday: Pat has just completed a telephone discussion with a customer and says aloud, "Nothing ever satisfies that guy!" Casey is walking by and says, "Better customer service is not as easy as you thought, huh?"

Monday morning staff meeting: Casey announces to the employees that any ideas for improvements or changes in business practices are welcome but should be submitted in writing, complete with the reasons for making the change, a cost analysis, and implementation details.

**What message do you think Pat received?**

_______________________________________________

_______________________________________________

*Compare your responses to the author's suggestions in the Appendix.*

## How Do You See Your Employees?

In the spaces below write the names or initials (or code words) of your employees and rate each one on the items listed.

5 = Excellent 4 = Very Good 3 = Good 2 = Fair 1 = Poor

**Name:**________________________________________

Taking initiative ___ Creativity ___
Problem solving ___ People skills ___
Working hard ___

**Name:**________________________________________

Taking initiative ___ Creativity ___
Problem solving ___ People skills ___
Working hard ___

**Name:**________________________________________

Taking initiative ___ Creativity ___
Problem solving ___ People skills ___
Working hard ___

**Name:**________________________________________

Taking initiative ___ Creativity ___
Problem solving ___ People skills ___
Working hard ___

The self-fulfilling prophecy will result in each of your employees continuing to be good at those things you rated 3, 4, or 5 and not improving upon those things you rated 1 or 2. Without being aware of it, you are probably sending subtle messages that reinforce their strengths and discourage their improving on their weaknesses.

## *Putting Self-Fulfilling Prophecy to Work*

Self-fulfilling prophecy is a particularly strong dynamic in the manager/employee relationship, as in any significant relationship in which one person wants and needs the approval, love, or acceptance of the other. What can you do to establish positive expectations in your relationships?

- Start looking for opportunities to notice employees doing something well that you previously thought was not among their strengths
- Provide training to help them develop in these areas
- Make a conscious effort to convey positive expectations about these characteristics and skills

## Case Study: A Positive Self-Fulfilling Prophecy

An executive who had just participated in a management development seminar and read a management improvement book learned about self-fulfilling prophecy. Still, the executive was skeptical about expectations being so powerful as to influence another's performance.

Deciding to test the phenomenon for himself, the executive chose an employee in his company to conduct his own experiment. He selected a young man who was a high school dropout working as a janitor. Stopping in the hallway one evening as he was leaving the building, he struck up a conversation with the young janitor. "Hi there. Your name is Peter, right?" "Yes, sir." He continued, "How do you like your job here, Peter?" "It's okay, sir." The executive then said, "You know, Peter, we are really short-handed in our Information Technology department and we could use a bright young man like you. How would you like to learn about computers?"

The janitor responded, "Gee, sir, I don't think I could learn about computers. I didn't even finish high school." "Well, Peter, I think you could do it! Come to my office on the 10th floor at 8:00 tomorrow morning and I will introduce you to the IT manager and get you started on a training program to learn data entry. You can learn that real fast and start making a much better wage."

The next morning the young man was introduced to the IT manager and a trainer who started teaching him data entry. Every couple of days the executive would drop in to ask Peter how he was doing and to compliment him on his abilities for learning this new job. Soon Peter was doing data entry and learning more about computers as his training continued. The executive still visited occasionally to check on Peter and congratulate him on his achievements. Now Peter is a computer programmer in his company.

*See the author's comments to this case study in the Appendix.*

# Creating Rapport

As important as positive expectations are for successful relationships, they are not the only component. As the manager you will also want to establish rapport with your employees.

Rapport is difficult to define because it is such an intangible thing that occurs between people. The dictionary describes it along the lines of "a harmonious accord." How would you define it?

______________________________________________

______________________________________________

______________________________________________

Many people describe rapport as a "connection" between people. Some say it is when two people "click" with each other and have the ability to communicate with ease. Indeed, rapport is that slippery phenomenon of somehow getting on the same communication frequency with one another with the result that we understand each other with seemingly little effort. Without rapport, communication is more strained.

How does rapport occur? How do you know when you have established rapport with someone?

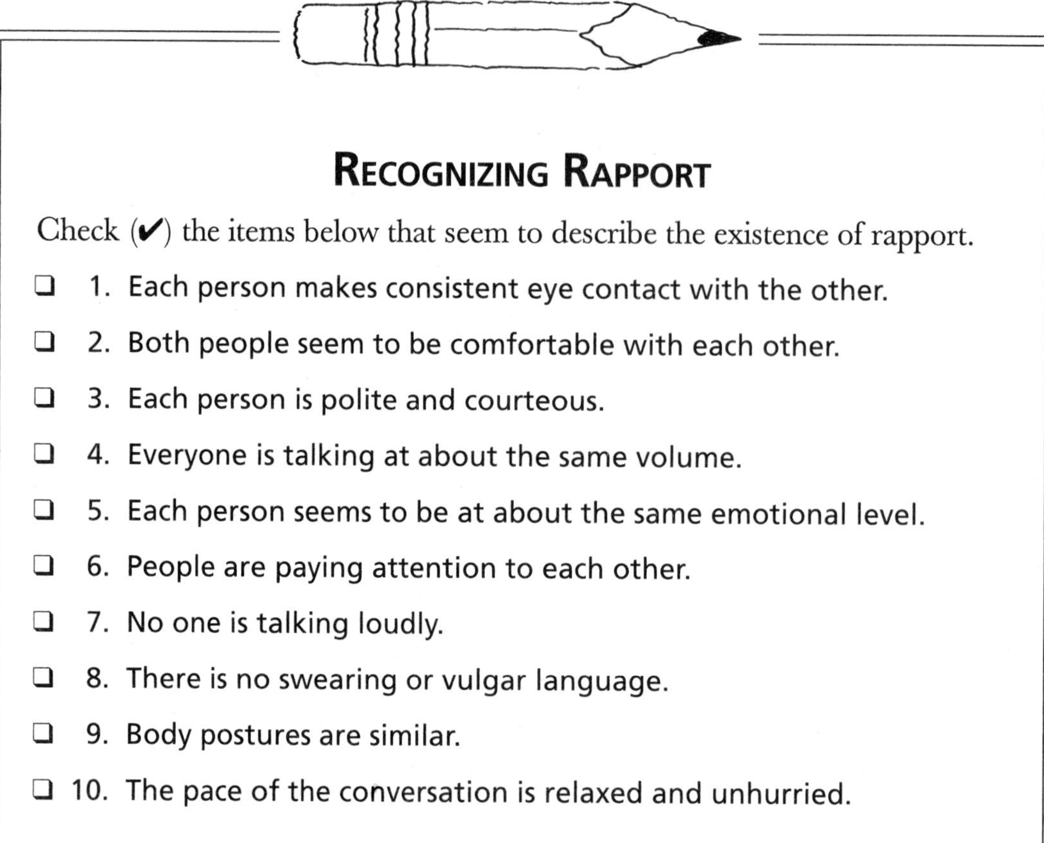

## Recognizing Rapport

Check (✔) the items below that seem to describe the existence of rapport.

❑ 1. Each person makes consistent eye contact with the other.

❑ 2. Both people seem to be comfortable with each other.

❑ 3. Each person is polite and courteous.

❑ 4. Everyone is talking at about the same volume.

❑ 5. Each person seems to be at about the same emotional level.

❑ 6. People are paying attention to each other.

❑ 7. No one is talking loudly.

❑ 8. There is no swearing or vulgar language.

❑ 9. Body postures are similar.

❑ 10. The pace of the conversation is relaxed and unhurried.

*Compare your responses to the author's suggestions in the Appendix.*

Cultural differences also play a part in rapport. In some cultures direct eye contact is considered impolite so its necessity for rapport applies only in those cultures that value direct eye contact, such as the United States, Canada, and many European countries. Even in the United States, however, exceptions exist. For example, men often carry on conversations while sitting or standing side-by-side rather than facing each other, limiting eye contact during the conversation.

Having rapport is like communicating by short-wave radio-you can communicate only when the sender and the receiver are using the same frequency. Likewise, when you and another person are "on the same frequency," you feel comfortable and connected with each other. You have rapport.

# Using the Pacing Technique

Most people depend upon rapport occurring accidentally–you have rapport with some people and you don't seem to have it with others. But you can also help create a connection with another person by practicing a technique known as *pacing*. This involves deliberately noticing certain characteristics of the other person and mirroring them, characteristics such as:

- **Pace or speed (slow or fast)**
- **Volume (soft, moderate, loud)**
- **Emotions**
- **Facial expressions**
- **Gestures, movements**
- **Body positions, postures**

A note about pace: Pay attention to how fast or slowly a person speaks and also notice his pace with other things. Does he want to talk business immediately or does he prefer to socialize a while first? Does she walk and move at a fast pace or more slowly? Does he answer questions immediately or does he take a few seconds to think before responding?

Why does mirroring personal characteristics help create rapport? Because we all are naturally most comfortable with people like ourselves. By making yourself more like those with whom you are communicating, you help them feel comfortable with you. It works. With a little practice you will notice people's traits more readily, and you will develop pacing skills-matching or mirroring just enough of their characteristics to increase rapport.

# Improving Listening Skills

Building and maintaining positive relationships depends on skillful listening. Unfortunately, most people receive little or no training in how to listen. Effective listening is more than just hearing-it involves specific skills. Let's check how you listen to others.

In response to the examples below, write what you would say or describe what you would do. Please write the actual words you would use if you were responding orally.

1. An employee says to you, "I just can't work with Pat! We seem to have a personality conflict. It doesn't matter what I say or do, we always end up spending half our time arguing instead of working on the project."

   **Your response:**

   ______________________________________________

   ______________________________________________

2. On another occasion, an employee says to you, "We sure waste a lot of time around here because we have to work with these outdated computers and old software. Are we ever going to upgrade?"

   **Your response:**

   ______________________________________________

   ______________________________________________

3. At another time, another employee says to you: "I thought I should let you know I'm considering some offers from other companies. The opportunities for promotion here seem to be pretty limited, and they are offering me some pretty attractive deals. I wanted to be fair and give you the chance to discuss my options if I stay here."

   **Your response:**

   ______________________________________________

   ______________________________________________

In each situation you might have been caught off guard, and most likely you responded in a way you couldn't even trace to having learned. Most of us receive no specific training in how to listen as we grow up, so most of our listening behaviors come from early role models. In the following exercise we'll evaluate common responses for possible reactions.

## Responding Effectively

Review the responses you wrote for the previous examples and check to see if your responses fall into any of the following categories. Circle the number of any responses that apply. Then we'll go back and evaluate the effectiveness of each response category.

| Type of response | Applies to which of your responses on page 18? | Potential negative reaction to your response |
|---|---|---|
| Advising, offering suggestions, telling the other what to do | 1 2 3 | |
| Explaining, being logical, giving facts or information | 1 2 3 | |
| Reassuring, sympathizing, consoling, encouraging | 1 2 3 | |
| Asking fact-finding questions, asking questions that can be answered either "yes" or "no" | 1 2 3 | |
| Criticizing, judging, blaming, being sarcastic or making a joke of their comments | 1 2 3 | |
| Preaching, lecturing, telling them what's best based on your own beliefs and standards | 1 2 3 | |
| Changing the subject, avoiding, withdrawing | 1 2 3 | |

CONTINUED

CONTINUED

| Type of response | Applies to Which of your responses on page 18? | Potential negative reaction to your response |
|---|---|---|
| Disagreeing, arguing, telling them they are wrong | 1 2 3 | |
| Agreeing, taking their side, complimenting or praising | 1 2 3 | |

Did you discover that your responses fit into one or more categories? Most people do. Most people learn the same listening responses that everyone else uses because that is how we heard people as we were growing up.

At this point you might be asking, "So, is there a problem with these responses?" The answer is sometimes yes. You can probably figure out for yourself what possible problems might be.

Now go back and describe what you think a possible negative reaction might be. Think how you would react if someone responded to you in this way. Also consider how your spouse or significant other might react if this were your response to something he or she said to you. How might each type of response result in a negative reaction or even cause a communication breakdown?

# Common Responses and Their Risks

| Response | Possible Negative Results |
|---|---|
| Advice, suggestions | Bad advice; "Yes, but" if unwanted; dependency |
| Explaining, facts, information | Seems uncaring/unconcerned, "you don't understand me" |
| Reassuring, sympathizing | Reinforces passivity, emotional dependency; heard as patronizing |
| Questioning | Other shuts down; puts focus on what you ask about (sidetracks) |
| Criticizing, judging | Other feels attacked; relationship may be damaged |
| Preaching, lecturing | Treats other as inferior; other is offended, shuts down |
| Changing subject, withdrawing | You don't care, other's needs unimportant, problem insignificant |
| Disagreeing, arguing | Creates conflict, discourages future interaction |
| Agreeing, complimenting | Reinforces bad decision; heard as insincere flattery |

All of the most common responses can produce a negative outcome, but that doesn't mean they are always the wrong things to say and do. Sometimes they create no problem at all. As a general rule, the common responses are most likely to have an undesired result when they are communicated to an emotional person. Then how do you respond to an emotional person?

# Diffusing Emotion Through Active Listening

The most effective response to an emotional person is what is often called active listening. Active listening takes place at three levels. They are:

**LEVEL 1** Attentiveness: eye contact, head nods, interested facial expression, responses such as "uh-huh," "yes," "I see," "I hear you."

**LEVEL 2** Door openers: prompting the other to talk, such as "tell me more," "go on," "then what happened?"

**LEVEL 3** Restatement of content and feelings: paraphrasing what the other just said and acknowledging his emotions (even if he didn't say what they are).

Levels 1 and 2 give the speaker the impression you are listening and that you are interested in what she is saying. You seem to care. Do these responses really prove to the speaker that you understood a word she said? No. They are appreciated by the speaker and will usually produce a positive reaction, but they do not demonstrate understanding. They also do not provide you, the listener, with any proof that what you have understood is correct.

Only Level 3, restatement of content and feelings, has any potential for proving that communication has actually occurred. When you paraphrase-not repeat word for word-what the speaker has just said, you prove to him that you understood. And when you acknowledge his feelings, you demonstrate your empathy-the ability to put yourself in the other's shoes, to get in touch with his emotions. Only Level 3 proves empathy and understanding. Few people know how to do it.

## *Listening with Empathy*

How does this paraphrasing sound with another person? Here are some examples:

**Speaker (employee):** *"Why do we have to break our necks to analyze all of this data every month? Nobody ever does anything with these reports anyway!"*

**Listener (manager):** *"You sound pretty frustrated with having to do work that doesn't seem to matter to anyone, right?"*

Notice how the listener acknowledged an unexpressed emotion–frustration–and restated the message without sounding like an echo by paraphrasing the words. Also notice how the response ends with a checkout question which prompts a response from the speaker. If the restatement is correct, the speaker will always say yes, and her emotional level will drop at least a little. The discussion continues:

**Employee:** *"Yeah, I am! We do all this work and no one ever says thank you and we never see any evidence that our information is ever used for anything!"*

**Manager:** *"It is a lot of work and it's disappointing to not hear a thank you now and then. I bet the others would also appreciate knowing how the reports are used, so I'll ask the regional manager to come to our next staff meeting to explain what the data is used for. Sound like a good idea?"*

This time the manager acknowledged feelings and the expressed need for recognition and information before proposing a solution for at least part of the problem. You can predict that the employee felt better for having been heard and will appreciate learning how hard work is being used for something important. When employees know they can be open and honest with their feelings and that their work is important, they are most likely to be accountable.

When the listening response demonstrates empathy and understanding, the employee will say more. Each time he says more, you learn more about him and the issue he has raised, which allows you to do a better job of working with him to reach a satisfactory conclusion. What might have seemed a difficult situation often turns out to be easier to resolve when you really listen and allow the employee time to come down emotionally from where he started.

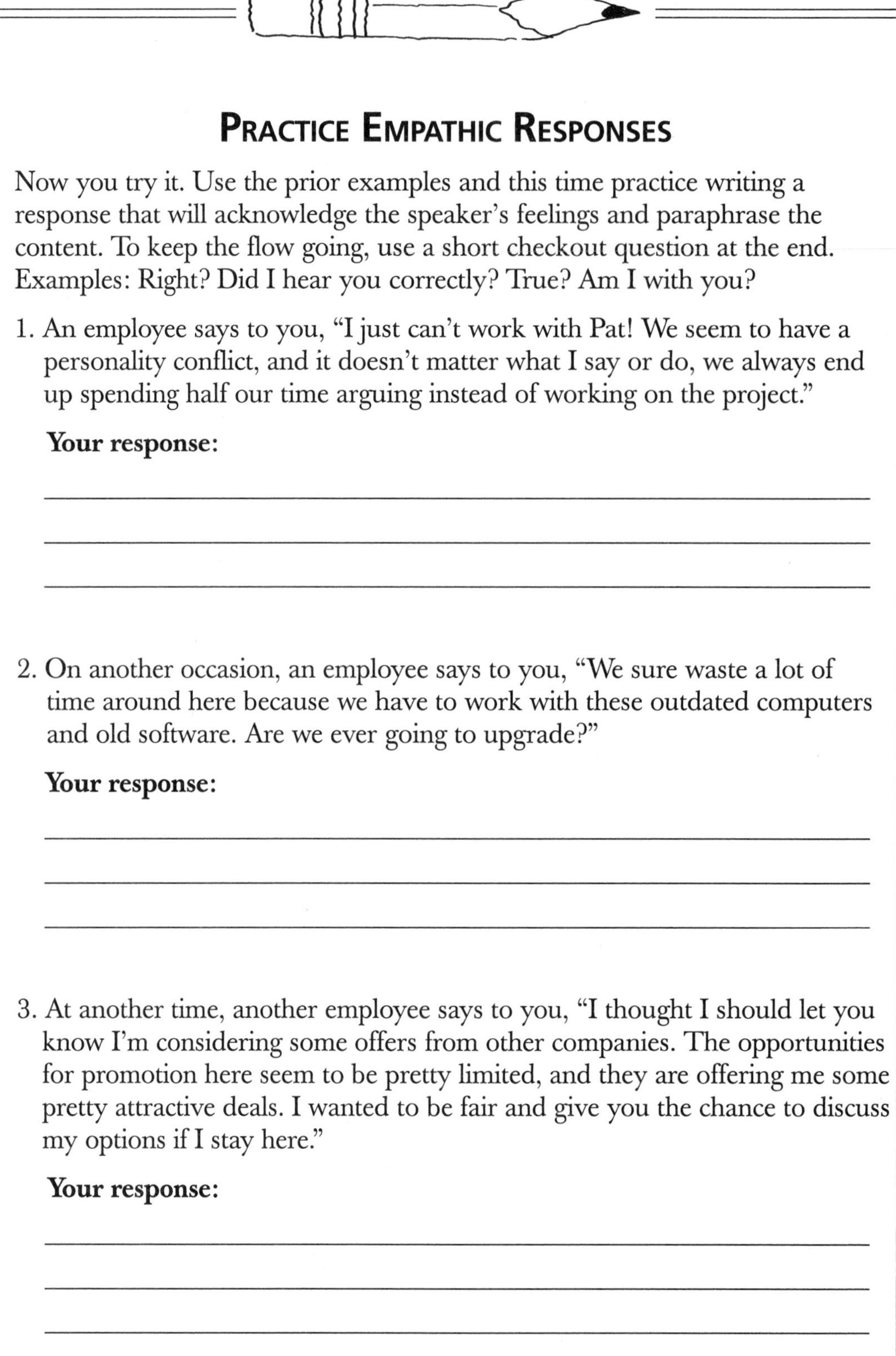

## Practice Empathic Responses

Now you try it. Use the prior examples and this time practice writing a response that will acknowledge the speaker's feelings and paraphrase the content. To keep the flow going, use a short checkout question at the end. Examples: Right? Did I hear you correctly? True? Am I with you?

1. An employee says to you, "I just can't work with Pat! We seem to have a personality conflict, and it doesn't matter what I say or do, we always end up spending half our time arguing instead of working on the project."

   **Your response:**

   ______________________________

   ______________________________

   ______________________________

2. On another occasion, an employee says to you, "We sure waste a lot of time around here because we have to work with these outdated computers and old software. Are we ever going to upgrade?"

   **Your response:**

   ______________________________

   ______________________________

   ______________________________

3. At another time, another employee says to you, "I thought I should let you know I'm considering some offers from other companies. The opportunities for promotion here seem to be pretty limited, and they are offering me some pretty attractive deals. I wanted to be fair and give you the chance to discuss my options if I stay here."

   **Your response:**

   ______________________________

   ______________________________

   ______________________________

*Compare your responses to the author's suggestions in the Appendix.*

# Lessening Employee Dependency

A major obstacle to better accountability is a problem that develops in most long-term relationships. *Overdependency* is very common in manager/employee relationships. If the participants do not learn how to resolve it, it can lead to the end of the relationship.

## *The Cycle of Dependency*

A pattern of dependency develops over time, without either party being aware. One person assumes the role of decision-maker and problem-solver while the other becomes more dependent upon the person filling those roles. In the beginning, this seems to work well because one person may have more experience or a natural talent for being in charge. The other person benefits because he doesn't have to learn what the decision-maker already knows.

Each person gets some needs met. The dominant one feels confident and competent and often enjoys solving problems, making decisions, and being in charge. The other person gets a problem solved without having to take time and expend energy learning how to do it himself, and he feels cared about.

Can you see where this pattern can lead? As the pattern continues, how will it affect the dominant person's self-esteem and her assessment of the other person and the relationship?

______________________________________________

______________________________________________

______________________________________________

How will the pattern affect the dependent person's self-esteem and his assessment of the other person and the relationship?

______________________________________________

______________________________________________

______________________________________________

## The Downward Spiral

In time the dominant person begins to resent the other's lack of initiative, inability to do things on his own, and constant need for help. The dominant person may begin to develop an inflated sense of her own importance. The dependent person is likely to doubt his own abilities and resent his powerless position or even fear what might happen if his partner weren't around some day to do things for him. Each person tends to blame the other–the dominant one saying, "... won't do it" and the dependent one saying, "... won't let me do it." Eventually the two people end up in a Rescuer/Victim relationship, which is unsatisfactory for both.

This dynamic is frequently underlying relationships that fail because one way to break the pattern is to end the relationship. A middle manager, for example, leaves his job because his boss is being controlling and reluctant to delegate important responsibilities. Realizing that he is slipping into a pattern of doing only what is required of him and showing little initiative, the middle manager is smart enough to realize he needs to get out of the situation if he is ever to develop his abilities.

## Promoting Accountability

Too many managers become "firefighters"-solving all the problems, making all the decisions, setting all the goals, and thinking of all the tasks to be done. Meanwhile, employees feel underused, unappreciated, disrespected, and uninvolved in decision-making, which results in their having little or no sense of ownership. Without ownership, employees feel minimal accountability.

What can you do to prevent overdependency and promote accountability? Take responsibility for your half of the relationship equation and improve your skills. Engage in active listening to help employees develop their own problem-solving skills. Delegate effectively to help foster ownership and maximum accountability. And learn how to invite others to hear you and interact with you as an equal. You will learn these skills in Part 3.

# Developing Relationship Contracts

Many managers assume that because an employee has accepted employment and has a job description that no further clarification of the manager's expectations is needed. This assumption often leads to problems. Conflicts occur when people interact based on unexpressed expectations, assumptions, and unequal power positions. But when all parties *know* what is expected of them, accepting responsibility and being accountable for the results are easier.

This is where the contractual approach to relationships comes in. The relationship contract does not replace the job description or the employment contract. It is an agreement between manager and employee that spells out performance objectives developed in discussions about goals, problems, needs, ambitions, and so on. Most of the problems that typically result from unexpressed expectations and unskillful delegation can be prevented when the manager and the employee develop an agreement about:

- **What the employee will do**
- **How the performance will be evaluated**
- **What rewards will be available**

## *A Valid Contract*

Relationship contracts can be oral, but putting them in writing adds to their importance and provides a document to use in performance discussions. With the written document, there can be no accusations of misunderstandings or poorly defined assignments. A good, workable contract includes four main elements:

- **Mutual Agreement**
- **Mutual Benefit**
- **Mutual Ability**
- **Legality**

Now let's look at each of these in more detail. Rather than engage in "legalese," we'll translate from a law text into everyday language. Including these four elements will help ensure clear expectations.

### Mutual Agreement

All parties must openly state their agreement to the terms. Silence does not mean agreement and head nods may not either. An oral or written agreement is required. One of the best ways to get this agreement is for one person to ask the commitment question, "Will you please ...?" and for the other to respond with "Yes" or "I will"–not "I'll try my best."

### Mutual Benefit

All parties must at least have the potential to gain from keeping the contractual commitment. When all parties understand that a positive payoff can result from keeping their commitment, they have much more incentive to do so. If parties are agreeing only to adapt to others or to get someone off their back, they are much less likely to keep their commitment.

### Mutual Ability

All parties must be able to do what they are committing to do. They must have the knowledge, skills, physical ability, resources, and time to allow them to carry out their part of the agreement. Don't just assume each other's ability but discuss what will be required of each person to ensure the contract works. A common problem with agreements in organizations is failing to ensure that this requirement is satisfied. For example, people often make unrealistic time commitments or claim to know more than they do because they want to please others and be perceived as team players.

### Legality

The contract must not violate the law, which can be interpreted to include national, state, and local laws; organizational policies or rules; and other existing agreements among the parties. If a contract does not comply with these laws and rules, then it will be unenforceable, which makes it much less effective.

A contract also must have a clearly defined starting date and ending date. This is more effective than an open-ended contract. It works better to use a defined time period and to renew the contract as needed and desired. This also requires the parties to evaluate their agreement periodically, which can foster improvements or even termination if it no longer satisfies the other requirements.

All of this may seem formal for everyday use, but think about the benefits of developing such a contract:

➢ **Everyone's needs are considered**

➢ **Each employee has a say in how things are done**

➢ **Each employee makes commitments to the others**

➢ **Communication is direct and open**

Makes sense, doesn't it? But most of us did not learn to deal with one another this way. It is another skill we have to develop. What you are learning in this book about goal setting, delegation, and positive reinforcement will help you negotiate effective performance contracts with your employees.

## Draft Your Own Contract

Choose an employee and think about what you hope this person will accomplish during a given time period. Do you have a specific project for this person? Would you like to delegate a significant responsibility? Has this person expressed a desire to learn something new, earn a promotion, or qualify for a raise?

In the spaces below fill in the information you could include in a performance contract. Ideally, you would develop these answers in discussions with the employee.

**The performance result to be achieved:**

______________________________________________

______________________________________________

______________________________________________

______________________________________________

**The reward/benefit to be earned with this accomplishment:**

______________________________________________

______________________________________________

**The time period: Start date: __________ Completion date: ____________**

**What laws/policies/rules might need to be checked to ensure the contract is *legal*?**

______________________________________________

______________________________________________

When people work out a clearly defined agreement–their commitments to one another, the potential benefits, and the performance requirements–before they even embark on the relationship or the project, they usually have many fewer disagreements and disappointments. Using the contractual approach also increases employees' commitment and responsibility for their own behavior and choices. Accountability is clearly defined and seldom becomes an issue.

# PART 3

# Leadership & Management Skills

# Defining Leadership

Most people think of a *leader* as someone with a vision who effectively communicates that vision to others who then help the leader achieve the vision. A leader is good at defining goals and inspiring others to achieve those goals. A leader is someone whom others trust and often admire.

How does a leader differ from a manager? The classic textbook definition of a *manager* is someone who gets things done through other people. This means the manager is responsible for accomplishing goals by making sure that other people carry out the action steps and tasks designed to produce the desired outcomes.

Do you see much difference between the two? Probably not. So why do people devote so much time, energy, and money to developing leadership abilities in managers? Because many managers don't have the skills for getting things done through other people. They become dictating bosses or paper shufflers or political creatures whose primary goal is to protect their jobs and further their careers by pleasing their own bosses. But a good manager is also a leader.

An effective manager gets things done by:

➢ **Involving employees in decisions**

➢ **Helping employees define goals and action plans**

➢ **Supporting and encouraging employees to do their best work**

➢ **Rewarding employees for good work and ideas**

➢ **Listening to employees and meeting their motivational needs**

➢ **Making sure that agreed-upon objectives are accomplished**

# Setting Goals to Communicate Your Vision

Leaders and good managers know the road to accomplishment starts with clearly defined goals, or objectives. So let's examine what goals are, the criteria for judging the quality of goals, and why goals are important for success.

Write in the space provided your definition of a goal:

____________________________________________________________

____________________________________________________________

A goal is a statement of an outcome you hope to achieve. It is a target result. It is not *what* you do–tasks–it is what you have when you have completed all the tasks.

Goals should be in writing to be most effective. When others are involved in meeting the goals, keeping the written goals visible to the team during the period it takes to achieve them helps everyone stay focused.

Writing goals is not as easy as many people think because high-quality goals must fit six basic criteria. These standards can be remembered by using the acronym SMARTS.

**Simple and specific.** Vague goals are not accomplished. Long statements full of big words are hard to understand and remember.

**Measurable.** The only way to know if the goal has been achieved is to be able to measure the outcome.

**Achievable.** Goals should be challenging but make sure they are realistic. Impossible goals lead only to failure and disappointment.

**Results.** A goal statement is not an action plan or a to-do list. You must state the goal as an outcome.

**Time limit.** Clearly defined time limits help counter procrastination. Long-term goals may need to be broken down into a series of short-term goals or checkpoints.

**Shared.** Because most accomplishments involve others in many ways, you will get maximum commitment and support by sharing the goal. Ideally, the others who will help you achieve the goal were also involved in determining the goal.

## Putting Your Goal in Writing

Try your hand at defining a goal that meets these standards. Think of something you want to accomplish and put it into words below.

____________________________________________________________

____________________________________________________________

____________________________________________________________

____________________________________________________________

Ask someone to read your goal statement and discuss how well it fits the SMARTS criteria.

**Simple/Specific**: Was the person able to understand what you intend to achieve just by reading what you wrote? If you had to explain, that suggests the goal as written could be improved.

**Measurable:** Did you indicate in your statement how you would measure the goal, or can you explain how you will do it? Remember, what gets measured gets done.

**Achievable:** Is your goal challenging and really possible?

**Results:** Did you write down a task or an outcome? This is often difficult to recognize. For example, exercising four days a week is an activity not a result. What is the outcome you hope to achieve?

**Time Limit:** Did you include a time limit in your goal statement and is it realistic? Without an achievable time limit, the goal may not be accomplished.

**Shared:** By asking someone to give you feedback about your goal statement, you have shared the goal with at least one person. You'll be most successful if you share it with others who can contribute to its accomplishment.

# Involving Employees to Create Buy-In

Many organizations and managers go through the motions of setting goals, but they often are not successful in involving employees. This ability to develop goals with employees involved separates effective managers from the mediocre. People who work to achieve goals they believe in are most likely to be accountable for their actions and decisions. Emphasize to employees, or the team, the importance of having their own goals related to those of the organization.

Ask your employees to write their own goal statements. People will be more strongly committed to goals they develop for themselves. Read and discuss your organization's objectives, then discuss how your department or team contributes to accomplishing the overall goals.

Most people are not taught about goals, and your job as their leader is to coach them. Discuss their statements to see that they satisfy the SMARTS criteria. Ask open-ended questions that prompt thinking. Here are questions to help employees improve their goal-setting skills:

### Questions to Help Define the Goal (Desired Outcome):

- What do you want to accomplish?
- What is the desired outcome?
- If you accomplish the desired outcome, what will you have?

### Questions to Help Determine the Measurement Criteria:

- How will you document your accomplishment?
- How will you know if you have achieved your goal?
- What measures will you use to track your progress?

### Questions to Help Explore Achievability:

- What are the challenges standing in the way of this goal?
- What problems do you anticipate?
- What might affect your ability to achieve this?

### Questions to Help Define the Time Required:

- When do you expect to have this goal completed?
- How much time will this take?
- What is your deadline?

# Determining the Action Steps

After writing and rewriting the goal statements for the best quality goals, the next step is to involve employees in determining the action steps that will lead to accomplishing the goals. Just as having ownership in goals fosters accountability, so does contributing to the plans for accomplishing the goals. Here are questions to facilitate this process:

## Questions to Help Define Action Steps:

- ➤ What will you need to help you accomplish this goal?
- ➤ From whom will you need cooperation to get this done?
- ➤ What ideas do you have about how to achieve your goal?
- ➤ What are some other possibilities?
- ➤ How else could you get the results you want?
- ➤ How can you get more ideas for developing your plans?

At this point you might be thinking, "But this will take so much time! It would be faster for me to just define the goals and action steps and assign the work to be done." True, it does take time to involve employees and have them define their own goals. But the reason for involving them is to increase their commitment to the goals and to foster ownership. Employees who are committed to goals with a feeling of ownership will always be more accountable than those who are expected to accomplish someone else's goals. And if you set goals for them, you are only encouraging overdependency as discussed in Part 2.

When employees have developed their own goals and action plans for the organization's success, they have maximum commitment to that success. Most employees do not have this opportunity, and the managers complain about their lack of motivation and loyalty. Is it really an employee problem or a management failure? By involving the employees in goal setting and planning, you can have a team of people with pride in their team, enthusiasm for their work, and maximum accountability for their actions and decisions.

# Empowering Employees Through Delegating

Managers often assign tasks when they delegate to their employees, rather than assigning responsibility for results. This does little to empower the employee with a sense of ownership. The effective manager knows that delegation is an important tool for empowering employees and adding to their job satisfaction and self-esteem.

Too often, however, the delegation is not handled skillfully, which results in confusion about what the employee is supposed to do. This usually leads to unsatisfactory results and conflict.

## *Why Is Delegation So Difficult?*

When managers are asked to identify the reasons they don't delegate, these are the most common answers:

➢ **I don't trust my employees.** Too many people still believe the old saying, "If you want something done right, do it yourself." Examine the reasons for your lack of trust in your employees, and then take the appropriate action to remove those reasons.

➢ **It takes longer to delegate than to do it myself.** This is often a rationalization because the actual time difference may be negligible. Even when the statement is true, the manager will probably have to do this same task again and again. Think of the time devoted to delegation as investing a little time today to save a lot of time in the future.

➢ **I enjoy doing it myself.** This is a common reason for holding on to jobs that could be delegated. Good managers know that they must look beyond their own preferences and consider what is best for accomplishing goals, for the entire organization, for the development of employees, and so on. As long as you are the only one who can do important tasks well, you are blocking your own advancement. If your bosses see no one prepared to step into your shoes, they cannot promote you.

- **I don't have anyone with experience or skills.** This is a good reason for being reluctant to delegate, but the solution is obvious-provide training.

- **I'm afraid they might do it better than I can.** Smart managers understand that you can't be the best at everything. You will impress people more by knowing how to use the strengths of your team than by trying to do everything yourself.

What other causes interfere with effective delegation? How can these challenges be resolved?

______________________________________________

______________________________________________

______________________________________________

______________________________________________

______________________________________________

______________________________________________

For many reasons managers of all levels fail to delegate skillfully. Regardless of your own reasons, you must recognize that being an effective manager means knowing when and how to delegate. Skillful delegation helps employees accept responsibility for being accountable for how they carry out the delegation.

## Case Study: Delegating or Dumping?

Marvin asks Tony and Ellen to join him in his office. He says to Tony, "The monthly production figures are too hard to use, and it's taking too much of my time to analyze all this stuff. Take this report and summarize each section for me. Also break out the comparison figures for the improvement over last year for each team. I'll want you to do this for me each month, Tony, okay?" Tony responds, "Uh, sure. I'll get right on it."

Marvin turns to Ellen and says, "Ellen, I've been getting lots of complaints from the shop supervisors that the support staff are uncooperative. They're going to have to understand that their job is to provide assistance to everyone and that includes the shop supervisors. I need you to get that across to them." He looks expectantly at Ellen who answers, "I'll talk to them in the staff meeting Monday, but I know they are going to complain that the shop supervisors don't give them enough time to..." Marvin interrupts Ellen and says, "I don't want to hear their excuses. I want you to make sure they start doing a better job! That's all. You both can get back to work now."

How do you rate Marvin's delegation skills?

Check (✔) each item below that you think he needs to improve.

- ❑ Instructions are specific and clear.
- ❑ The employee is given enough authority to do the job.
- ❑ The manager confirms that the employee understood accurately.
- ❑ The employee is given authority to make decisions and suggestions.
- ❑ Responsibility for results rather than a specific task is delegated.
- ❑ The employee receives encouragement and positive expectations.
- ❑ A system for follow-up evaluation is established.
- ❑ The employee is encouraged to ask clarifying questions.

*Compare your responses to the author's suggestions in the Appendix.*

## Preparing To Delegate

An effective manager knows that delegation is a complex skill that requires preparation and good communication skills. To improve your delegation skills, answer the following questions before each delegation:

### 1 What is the goal or objective of delegating this task or responsibility?

Answering this question identifies the delegation's expected outcome. This will help you to delegate a responsibility for outcome rather than just a meaningless task.

**Example:** Marvin could have defined his delegation goal as redesigning the production reports to produce information that could be used without so much additional analysis.

**Practice:** Define the delegation goal for the problem that was given to Ellen in the earlier example.

______________________________________________

______________________________________________

### 2 Whom will I select for this assignment?

This question requires you to consider your candidates. Who is the most qualified? Who would most like to do this? Who needs the growth experience? Who has the time? Who could handle this with some training?

**Example:** Marvin might have selected Tony because he is familiar with production, likes working with numbers, and has a good relationship with the production team.

**Practice:** What factors might Marvin have considered in choosing Ellen for the other delegation?

______________________________________________

______________________________________________

## 3 What kind of authority or power is needed and how much is required?

This answer is important if the person is to be empowered enough to be successful. Assigning a responsibility without giving appropriate power will almost always guarantee failure.

**Example:** Marvin would need to give Tony authority to ask the production people for different data, to experiment with different formats, and possibly to call upon people in other departments such as accounting, quality assurance and data processing for assistance.

**Practice:** What authority would Ellen need for her assignment?

______________________________________________________________

______________________________________________________________

## 4 Who else needs to know about this delegation?

Your employee has authority only when others know that you have given this power. Think about all who may be involved in carrying out this delegation and inform each one about it.

**Example:** To assure Tony's success, Marvin would need to inform the production crew, accounting, quality assurance and data processing that Tony has authority to request their help with the project.

**Practice:** Who would need to know about Ellen's assignment and the extent of her authority?

______________________________________________________________

______________________________________________________________

## 5 What type of control or feedback will I need?

A major concern about delegating is the loss of control, so you need to figure out how you can reduce this stress factor. What kind of information will you want about progress and how often? How will you meet your need for control so you avoid looking over your employee's shoulder (which communicates distrust)?

**Example**: Marvin might want Tony to discuss new format designs with him before implementing them. He might want a weekly progress report.

**Practice:** What controls or feedback would Marvin want in Ellen's case?

___

___

## 6 What is a reasonable time limit for completion?

You may want to involve the employee in answering this question. A clear deadline helps to focus efforts and increases the probability of success. The time limit needs to be realistic for both your needs and your employee's.

**Example**: For Tony's assignment, a reasonable time limit might be several months or longer to allow for experimentation with different reporting formats and for developing the computer programming. It could take longer, depending on the amount of data needed and the complexity of the redesign challenge.

**Practice:** What would be a reasonable time limit for Ellen's assignment of resolving the conflict between the shop supervisors and the support staff?

___

___

## 7 When and how will we evaluate the performance?

Planning for evaluation ensures you will identify the measures of success and arrange a system for providing the information needed for evaluation. The employee deserves positive reinforcement of a good performance and coaching assistance with any problems.

**Example:** Marvin and Tony will need to evaluate how well the new reporting system provides the needed data. They also will want to evaluate how Tony went about resolving the problem. The evaluation might include asking others who were involved to evaluate Tony's role.

**Practice:** What aspects of Ellen's performance will need to be evaluated and how might this be done?

___

___

Planning for delegation is essential to ensure the assignment will be completed successfully. Delegation is an important opportunity to strengthen your relationship with employees and to empower them so that everyone benefits.

## The Delegation Discussion

The next major step in delegation is communicating with the person selected for the assignment. Use the following guidelines to assist you with this important communication challenge:

- Meet face-to-face without time pressure. Memos and e-mail messages are more likely to be misunderstood than oral give and take. Allow time for questions and to discuss alternatives. Summarize the agreements in writing after the meeting.

- Ask rather than command. Most people prefer to be asked rather than told what to do. It is a subtle demonstration of respect. Asking also requires a response from the employee while a command does not.

- Check for understanding and commitment. Don't ask, "Do you understand?" or "Okay?" because most people will say yes even when they don't clearly understand. Ask the employee to summarize what you have discussed. You must receive a definite commitment; don't accept "I'll try" because this answer signals a potential failure. Remember self-fulfilling prophecy? Someone who says, "I'll try," does not expect to succeed.

- Agree on the control procedures and the follow-up date. If you and the employee agree about how you will be kept informed, you will not need to check up. If you both know in advance when and how the performance will be evaluated, the delegation is more likely to be successful. This agreement about control and follow-up also helps communicate your expectation that the employee is accountable for the results.

Inform others about the delegation. Your delegation is not complete until you have told everyone who may be affected or involved.

## Case Study: Delegating to Empower

Marvin asks Tony to join him in his office. "Tony, I'm having trouble using the production figures. I have to spend too much time analyzing the data. I know you are familiar with production and that you are good with numbers. You also have a solid relationship with the production people, so I would like you to figure out a better way to report this information. Are you willing to take this on?"

Tony responds, "I would love to! What are the biggest problems with the way the information is reported now?"

Marvin answers, "I can't tell at a glance how each team is doing on production goals or in comparison to the other teams. I also have to spend a lot of time looking up last year's performance figures to check our improvement."

Tony says, "Okay, that gives me a better idea of what you need. May I get some help from Sherry in data processing? She is our best programmer and I'll bet she'll have some good ideas about how to get this data reported in more useful ways."

Marvin answers, "Sure, Tony, and I'll authorize whatever computer time you two will need. I'll also tell all of the production people that you are going to need their cooperation. Anything else?" Tony says, "Not right now, but I may have more questions later." Marvin ends with, "Ask anytime, Tony. Will you give me a weekly progress report and present your ideas to me before we make any changes in the system?" "Sure, boss."

*See the author's comments to this case study in the Appendix.*

## DO YOUR OWN DELEGATION

Write down your ideas about how to delegate the other assignment to Ellen and practice with a friend or family member.

# Recovering and Learning from Mistakes

One of the challenges in fostering maximum accountability is responding to the employee who makes a mistake. Managers in organizations of all types and sizes too often respond to mistakes in a disapproving or punitive manner. Such a response has a detrimental effect on accountability. When mistakes result in rebukes, ridicule, interrogation, or punishment, employees learn to fear making mistakes. Old behavior patterns such as making excuses, denying responsibility, and blaming others get reinforced. This is the opposite of being accountable.

## *The Cost of Mishandling Mistakes*

When mistakes result in angry lectures, suspension or probation, reductions in income, written documentation of poor performance, or even termination of employment–all common responses–an unwritten rule is being communicated to employees: never make mistakes. Is this realistic? Of course not, but this perception exists in most organizations and work groups. When this is the unwritten expectation, how do employees approach their work? ____________________

____________________________________________________________

If you said cautiously or fearfully, you know the consequence of treating mistakes harshly. Yet time and again, employees receive only punitive responses. No wonder so many resist change and efforts to improve. They know that changing things increases the probability of making mistakes, and they are not going to take that chance if they don't have to. Why set oneself up for punishment?

Possibly the biggest price organizations pay for treating mistakes punitively is the lesson employees learn about making a mistake. What do people learn to do about a mistake they have made? ______________________________

____________________________________________________________

Everyone knows the answer is cover it up. Rather than be accountable for their actions, employees are taught to be anxious about making mistakes and to protect themselves from punishment by hiding the ones they do make. Why do managers continue to handle mistakes so badly when the cost to themselves and the organization is so obvious? The simple answer is that no one has taught them how to do it better. All of our lives we have been criticized by parents, teachers, and our own bosses for making mistakes. How were we supposed to learn a positive, helpful way to treat the mistakes of others?

## Case Study: One Mistake Leads to Another

Tony and Sherry have responded enthusiastically to their challenge and have generated many ideas about how to improve the production reporting. They have designed a new form for the supervisors to use in reporting the information to data processing, so they will have what they need for a newly designed report to Marvin. Predictably, the supervisors are resistant to changing and have complained to the production manager. The production manager tells Marvin, "Tony has my supervisors in an uproar, Marvin. They are complaining to me about all these new forms and they don't understand why we're always changing things!"

Marvin encounters Tony in the hallway talking with Sherry and two other employees and says angrily, "Tony, I told you not to change any forms until you had cleared your ideas with me! You've got everyone in production mad. Not only have you not helped me with my problem-you've created a bigger one!"

A familiar scene? Tony has made a mistake but Marvin has made an even bigger one, hasn't he? What are Marvin's mistakes?

_______________________________________________

_______________________________________________

_______________________________________________

_______________________________________________

*Compare your responses to the author's suggestions in the Appendix.*

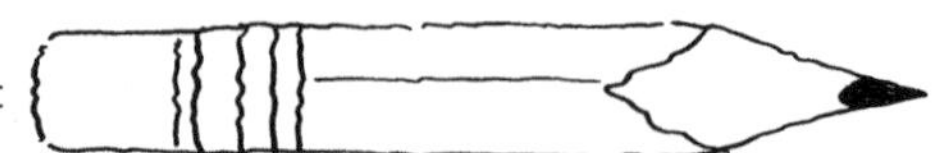

## Reacting to Mistakes

Recall your own mistakes and check (✔) each of the experiences below that were unpleasant for you.

- ❑ Feelings of self-disgust
- ❑ Anger about wasted time
- ❑ Fear of discovery
- ❑ Embarrassment
- ❑ Rebuke by boss, parent, or other
- ❑ Teasing by friends, peers
- ❑ Public reprimand
- ❑ Being asked for an explanation
- ❑ Lack of coaching help
- ❑ Punishment

You may have checked several choices because different mistakes produce different outcomes, and each person reacts differently to each response. Now reconsider those you checked and decide which one or two you dislike most and circle those. Do you think others might react similarly?

## *Coaching Employees Through Their Mistakes*

Making mistakes is inevitable. But how you handle your employees' mistakes will make a difference in how they accept responsibility in the future. The successful manager knows that mistakes are opportunities for coaching employees to:

- Identify the cause of the mistake
- Determine corrective actions
- Learn how to prevent the recurrence of the same mistake
- Be more comfortable being accountable

Coaching employees through their mistakes is a step-by-step process that helps employees learn from their mistakes and helps managers improve their working relationships. Follow this sequence for best results:

### 1 Demonstrate respect, care, and reassurance.

The employee already feels bad about making a mistake. Say or do nothing to communicate disapproval. Show you care with statements such as "Everybody makes mistakes," "Don't punish yourself," "You just proved you're human."

### 2 Share one of your own mistakes.

Tell the employee about one of your own mistakes to help him feel better and to build trust in your relationship. People are less likely to hide mistakes when they know you have made them too.

### 3 Ask one question and listen.

Ask an open-ended question such as "What happened?" or "How did this happen?" Keep quiet and allow time for the other to answer. If the employee is going to learn from this mistake, she must do most of the thinking. By telling you how the mistake occurred, she will be more likely to remember what was done incorrectly. Do not ask a series of fact-finding questions because you will be doing all of the thinking. Your goal is to help employees learn to ask their own questions and think for themselves.

## 4 Ask another question and listen.

When the employee has identified what was done incorrectly, you ask, "How can you fix it?" Again, allow the other person to do the thinking. When employees think of solutions, they are much more likely to remember them and follow through than if you do it for them. If they don't know how, work together to identify possible alternatives.

## 5 Ask a final question and listen.

To help ensure the same mistake will not be repeated, ask, "How can you make sure this won't happen again?" Allow time for an answer, listen, and restate. When employees themselves figure out the actions needed to prevent recurrence, they are more likely to learn from the experience.

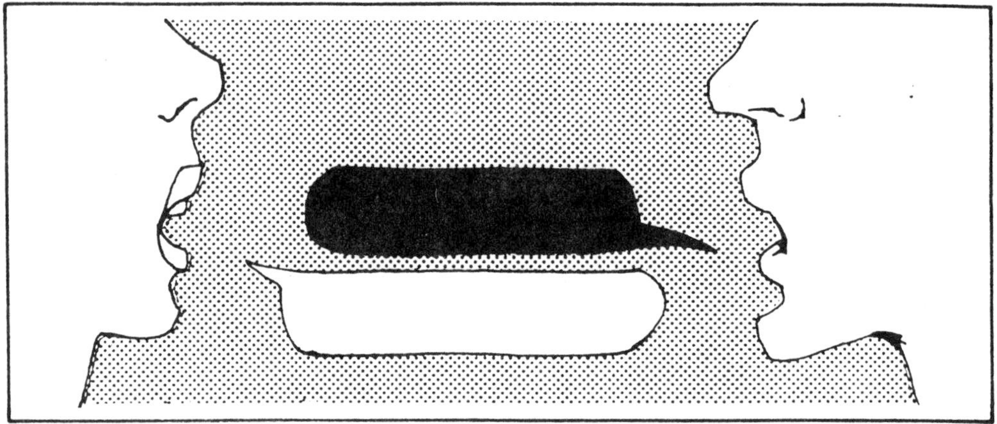

## Case Study: A Positive Learning Experience

Marvin learns from the production manager that Tony has designed new forms for the supervisors to report production results and that they are unhappy about all of the changes. He finds Tony in the hallway talking with Sherry and two other co-workers. He says, "Tony, when you finish here, will you check with me in my office?"

"Sure, Marvin. We just finished and I want to tell you about what Sherry and I have done anyway."

When Tony and Marvin return to Marvin's office, Marvin says, "Before you tell me about your project, let me share something with you. Franklin was just in here telling me about your new forms and how the supervisors are resisting the changes. I'm unhappy about this because I thought we agreed you would clear any new forms with me before implementing them. Was that our agreement?"

"Uh, yeah, I guess I got excited about our ideas and forgot to check it out with you. I'm sorry."

"That's okay, Tony. We all make mistakes. I remember that my first week on the job here I got so excited about the project I was working on that I did some work that was only supposed to be done by someone with security clearance. I had the security team all over me!"

"You're kidding!"

"Nope. I really did. So you're telling me that in your excitement you just forgot to clear your ideas with me and I can understand that. How can you get the supervisors to calm down and work with you on this?"

"I think it would be a good idea for me to tell them that I jumped the gun a little and apologize for not communicating with you and them about our ideas before presenting them with a new form."

Marvin responds, "That might do it, Tony. Would you like for me to help you out by meeting with all of you to provide moral support? About all I would say is that you are helping me to figure out ways to make our reporting more useful." (Pause) "How can you make sure something like this won't happen again?" Tony answers, "I think it would be a good idea for me to meet with you each week to discuss our progress rather than submitting a written report like I was doing." Marvin says, "Good idea. Let's do it."

*See the author's comments to this case study in the Appendix.*

*P A R T* **4**

# Communication Tools That Build Accountability

# Matching Personality Type

As you have learned, effective leadership depends on communication. When you communicate effectively with employees, they are more likely to feel trusted and respected by you and to want to honor their commitments to you. The result is maximum accountability.

This leads us back to the need for rapport, the foundation of effective communication. And one of the best ways to build rapport with someone is to match that person's dominant personality type, or style. This is an advanced application of the pacing technique you learned in Part 2.

Personality types can be described in numerous ways, and personality assessment instruments can provide detailed feedback about a person's primary and supporting personality characteristics. But you need not test people or conduct a psychological interview to learn someone's personality type. Once you know what to look and listen for, you can learn to identify a person's dominant type or style by simply paying attention to the person for a little while.

## *The Four Personality Types*

Four major personality types are found in all cultures around the world. Each person possesses at least a little of each type but one is dominant. It is this dominant set of characteristics that you need to recognize when interacting with someone. The four types are:

- **Directing/Guiding**
- **Supporting/Caring**
- **Analytical**
- **Expressive**

Each person's dominant type provides important personality clues including one's natural communication style. On the next page are clues to recognizing each type.

**Directing/Guiding** personalities operate at a fast pace in an authoritative/commanding style. They have strongly held beliefs that they discuss with passion. They tend to believe that their values and standards are what everyone should follow. Directing/Guiding people prefer to keep things impersonal, and are not comfortable with closeness and emotional interaction. They focus on action, results, and the bottom line. They tend to look serious, use powerful gestures, exhibit more rigid posture, and speak more rapidly and loudly than others. Famous Directing/Guiding personalities include General Patton, Margaret Thatcher, Ross Perot, and Lee Iacocca.

**Supporting/Caring** personalities are recognized by their slower pace and their warm, nurturing style. They value relationships and work hard to build and maintain relationships with others. They are thoughtful and giving with other people. Supporting/Caring people are the ones to whom others turn when they have troubles and need "a shoulder to cry on." They come across as gentle, kind and approachable. They smile a lot, look friendly and gentle, display relaxed and open postures, touch others in a comforting manner, and speak more slowly and softly. Well-known personalities in this group are Barbara Bush, Mr. Rogers, Bob Keeshan (Captain Kangaroo), and Oprah Winfrey.

**Analytical** personalities also exhibit a slower pace, but in an unemotional, formal, logical style. They value information, accuracy, timeliness, and clear thinking. Like the Directing type, Analyticals prefer interaction with others to be impersonal. They are most comfortable with one-on-one communication and want to talk about facts, figures, timelines and concepts. They show little facial expression (poker face); keep gestures to a minimum; and speak in a careful, measured pace, using more sophisticated and complex word choices in long sentences. Well-known Analyticals include Al Gore, Peter Jennings, Diane Sawyer, Alan Greenspan, and Hillary Clinton.

**Expressive** people are recognized by their fast pace and emotional, energetic, animated style. They value excitement, fun, creativity, and being different from others. They are proud of their uniqueness and individuality. They enjoy being with people and like things to be lively and fast-paced. They thrive on attention and they get a lot of it with their flamboyant style. Expressives are animated and energetic, with the widest range of facial expressions, which shift frequently. They speak rapidly with quite a bit of emotion, change postures often, and react spontaneously to what others say and do. Robin Williams, Jim Carrey, Carol Burnett, Dennis Rodman, and Madonna are famous Expressives.

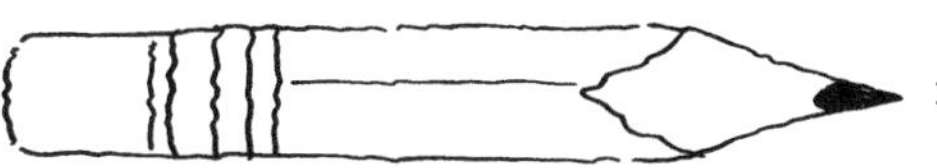

## Name That Type

With just this brief introduction to the four groups, practice identifying the communication style of each in the examples below. Write in the letter for the personality type that fits each example.

D = Directing/Guiding S = Supporting/Caring A = Analytical E = Expressive

___ 1. I see the total dollar sales, but what is the percentage increase over last year's sales?

___ 2. Cool! We sold that much stuff?

___ 3. The best way to improve profits is to cut costs to the bone.

___ 4. Give me just five minutes with that guy, and I'll tell him what to do to fix this problem.

___ 5. I really wish we could get this done without hurting anyone's feelings.

___ 6. The most important criterion is whether the solution is cost-effective.

___ 7. When's lunch?!

___ 8. Is your stomach all you can think about?! Get serious and help solve this problem.

___ 9. Now, Val, don't be mean to Terry.

___ 10. It would seem that the current situation is at least partially influenced by the history of the relationship with this particular client.

___ 11. I agree. Client relationships are the key to our success; we need to make sure clients are happy with our products and service.

___ 12. We make good products and we give good service. Some clients just like to complain.

*Compare your responses to the author's suggestions in the Appendix.*

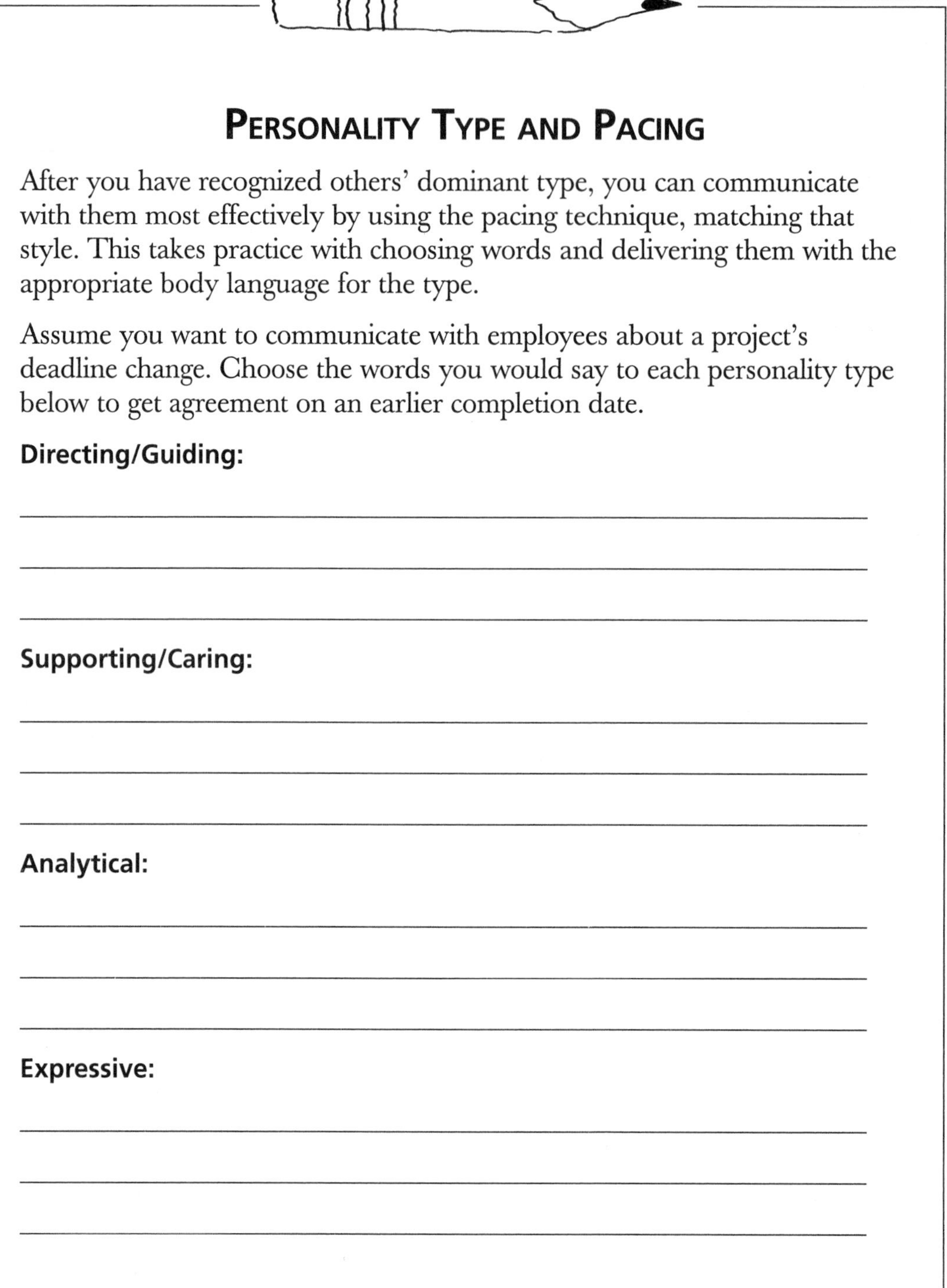

## Personality Type and Pacing

After you have recognized others' dominant type, you can communicate with them most effectively by using the pacing technique, matching that style. This takes practice with choosing words and delivering them with the appropriate body language for the type.

Assume you want to communicate with employees about a project's deadline change. Choose the words you would say to each personality type below to get agreement on an earlier completion date.

**Directing/Guiding:**

______________________________________________

______________________________________________

______________________________________________

**Supporting/Caring:**

______________________________________________

______________________________________________

______________________________________________

**Analytical:**

______________________________________________

______________________________________________

______________________________________________

**Expressive:**

______________________________________________

______________________________________________

______________________________________________

*Compare your responses to the author's suggestions in the Appendix.*

## *Delegating to Personality Type*

It is almost magical how much more effective your communications can be when you recognize and match the other person's natural personality type. Apply this rapport-building skill as you delegate, and you will see your employees understand you more accurately and trust you more. To delegate most effectively to a:

- **Directing/Guiding person**–Be direct and to the point and tell the employee what results you expect and when you expect them. Tell her to give you progress reports at specified times. Tell her how the assignment makes an impact and give positive feedback about the quality of work done.

- **Supporting/Caring person**–Take a few minutes with the employee to chat about family or a personal interest and then ask for his help. Explain what results you need and when you need them and ask for progress reports at specified times. Let him know how much you appreciate being able to depend upon him. When the results are achieved, thank him and give positive feedback about how much the results have helped you.

- **Analytical person**–Make an appointment with the employee to discuss the assignment. Provide plenty of information about the objectives to be achieved, the reasons for selecting her for the assignment, and the time for completion. Ask her if she will agree to accept the assignment. Request progress reports at specified times, and be prepared to give positive feedback about the accuracy and timeliness of the completed work.

- **Expressive person**–Let the employee know you have a special assignment he will enjoy. Let him know you chose him because of his energy and enthusiasm. Agree upon frequent progress reports and give him lots of positive feedback about how well he is doing. When the results have been achieved, talk about what a great job he did and be genuinely enthusiastic.

When you strengthen your rapport by matching people's dominant personality type, they are more comfortable with you, which leads to increased accountability in their relationship with you.

# Communicating Win-Win Messages

Whenever one person speaks or writes to another, two messages are communicated–the thoughts, opinions, feelings, and information of the message itself and a statement about the sender's worth and the receiver's worth. This dynamic is sometimes referred to as an ego message. People use one of these three behavior types, each of which communicates a different ego message:

- **Nonassertive**
- **Aggressive**
- **Assertive**

Every time we interact with others, we have the opportunity to strengthen the relationship or weaken it through the ego messages we communicate. Only one of these behavior types communicates the win-win ego message that says, "I'm OK and you're OK, too." Let's look at the three types in more detail:

## Nonassertive

The message of nonassertive behavior is "I'm not OK; you're OK," which invites others to perceive themselves as superior while seeing the communicator as inferior. This behavior is passive, indirect, and ineffective. It usually leads to win-lose outcomes with the nonassertive person being the loser.

People choose nonassertive behavior because of low self-esteem, feeling threatened (the flight or freeze response to threat), perceiving others as more important, trying to avoid hurting someone's feelings, wanting to please others, or uncertainty about the accuracy or validity of the communication. Why else might someone choose nonassertive behavior?

______________________________________________________________________

______________________________________________________________________

______________________________________________________________________

______________________________________________________________________

## Aggressive

The message of aggressive behavior is "I'm OK; you're not OK," which invites others to perceive themselves as inferior. It also invites others to perceive the communicator as superior, but others are just as likely to see the communicator as arrogant, condescending, rude, demanding, or downright mean and nasty. This behavior is likely to be direct and active, but it can be indirect and passive. It creates win-lose outcomes with the aggressive person winning at the expense of someone else.

People are aggressive because they believe they are superior, want to control the situation, feel threatened (the fight response to threat), are retaliating for past mistreatment, are stressed or feeling bad, lose emotional control, or are convinced they are right and someone else is wrong. Why else might someone choose aggressive behavior?

________________________________________

________________________________________

________________________________________

________________________________________

## Assertive

The message of assertive behavior is "I'm OK; you're OK," which invites others to feel respected and to respect the communicator-win-win communication. This behavior is direct, active, socially appropriate, and respectful. Rather than being controlling, assertive behavior is influencing. When we are assertive we do not intimidate; we negotiate. Why might someone choose assertive behavior?

________________________________________

________________________________________

________________________________________

________________________________________

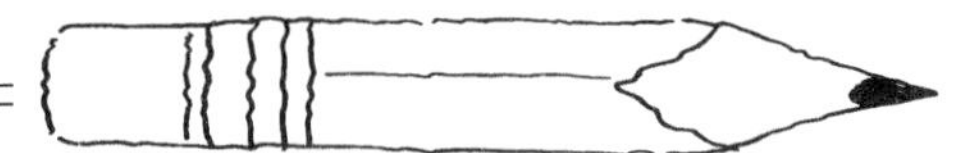

## Win, Lose, or Win-Win

Practice recognizing these three kinds of behavior in the examples below by writing the abbreviation in the space provided.

NAS = Nonassertive AS = Assertive AG = Aggressive

___ 1. Will you please arrange a meeting with Fred and Sue?

___ 2. If you would think before you speak, then you wouldn't make such stupid mistakes.

___ 3. Give me a hand with this thing.

___ 4. Do you think you might be able to see your way clear to approve my request?

___ 5. Why don't you just move it over there instead of walking around it all of the time?

___ 6. I'm not sure this is quite what you had in mind but I hope it will work. Okay?

___ 7. Oh, sure, I'll do it over if you think it would be better. It was stupid of me not to think of that.

___ 8. I'm concerned about making a good impression with this new client. How do I look?

___ 9. Look, just say what you mean, why don't you?

___ 10. You did an excellent job with the presentation.

___ 11. You know, it would be nice if we could kind of discuss this without getting personal.

___ 12. Wow! We did it!

___ 13. Big deal! We've done better.

___ 14. I guess that will be okay. I mean, if everyone else thinks it's okay.

___ 15. Don't forget to get your expenses turned in by Friday. And do it right this time, okay?

*Compare your responses to the author's suggestions in the Appendix.*

## *Body Language Speaks Volumes*

Word choices are not the only way to tell if someone is being nonassertive, assertive, or aggressive. Ego messages also are communicated non-verbally, through body language. Here are the non-verbal signals most often associated with each behavior type.

| Nonassertive | Assertive | Aggressive |
|---|---|---|
| Chin lowered | Head level | Chin raised |
| Shoulders forward | Shoulders straight | Shoulders back |
| Elbows close to body | Arms relaxed | Elbows out |
| Nervous-looking movements | Relaxed movements | Abrupt, tense movements |
| Hand wringing, twisting | Open gestures | Finger pointing, chopping motion |
| Low volume, soft-spoken | Moderate volume | Loud or moderate with tension |
| Little or no eye contact | Direct eye contact | Piercing eye contact or none |
| Halting delivery | Steady delivery | Staccato delivery |

Additional signals may have different meanings in different cultures. Different cultures also have different standards for what is perceived as socially appropriate and respectful, so do some research before interacting with people from a culture different from your own.

## Case Study: Accountability through Communication

Terry is seated at a conference table waiting for several employees to arrive for a meeting. When people arrive they say hello. Each time, Terry returns the greeting without looking up from his papers. When all are present he says, "The plant manager is not happy with the latest productivity report, and I'm supposed to recommend some improvements, so I thought it might be a good idea for us to kind of do some brainstorming. You know, just go around the table a few times to see if we could sort of generate a few ideas to improve productivity. Can anyone maybe think of something to get us started?" The employees look uncertain and glance at one another to see if someone will speak first. After a few seconds of silence, Terry shrugs and says, "Oh well, if you don't have any ideas right now, that's okay. Why don't you give it some thought, and if you have some ideas, just jot them down or something and give them to me later. Okay?" He looks back down at his papers. One employee slowly stands up and asks, "Shall we go back to work now?" Terry looks up just briefly with a look of surprise and answers, "Oh! Uh, yeah, sure. Let me know if you think of anything."

Which behavior type was Terry exhibiting?____________________

Morgan bursts into the meeting room and says loudly, "Okay. We don't have much time for this meeting because we have to get back to work, but the plant manager is ticked off about the last productivity reports and wants ideas for improvement. He 'suggested' that we have brainstorming sessions with our teams and get back to him with ideas by next week. So give me some ideas!" While sitting down at the head of the conference table where the employees had left an empty seat, Morgan looks sternly at each person around the table. The employees one by one lower their eyes and say nothing. After a few seconds Morgan exhales loudly and says, "I knew it was a dumb idea to try brainstorming with people who aren't paid to think, but at least I can tell the boss we had a meeting! Okay, get back to work." The employees all jump up and scurry from the room with looks of relief.

Which behavior type was Morgan exhibiting?____________________

Kelly walks into the meeting room, looks around the room to make eye contact with each person, smiles, and greets each one by name. Kelly takes a seat on the side of the table next to an employee and says, "The plant manager is not very happy with our latest productivity figures and has asked each of us managers to have brainstorming sessions with our teams to generate some ideas for improvement. You are all familiar with the brainstorming rules, but let's review them to make sure we follow the procedure. Jim, will you remind us of the ground rules?" After Jim recites the rules and writes them on the whiteboard, Kelly says, "Since I have had a little time to think about this, I'll toss out the first idea, and then we can keep going around the table until we run out of ideas. We'll call time after 15 minutes if we are still going because we have to get back to work." Kelly offers an idea and then asks, "What do you think would help improve productivity?" ... After 15 minutes of spirited and enthusiastic discussion that produces a couple dozen ideas, Kelly says, "Okay. Time for us to stop. Terrific job, team! If it's okay with you, I'll go through all of these and cull the ones that are a little silly (the group laughs) or too costly for immediate consideration and prepare a report for the plant manager. I think we have some really good suggestions. Thanks again!"

Which behavior type was Kelly exhibiting?____________________

---

Consider the three managers' handling of the brainstorm sessions and answer the following questions.

Which manager do you think is perceived by the team as an effective leader, and why?________________________________________

__________________________________________________

Which manager do you think the team believes would support them to upper management if things went wrong? Why? Why might they not expect the same support from each manager?______________________________

__________________________________________________

What would you predict about the level of accountability within each manager's team?________________________________________

__________________________________________________

*Compare your responses to the author's suggestions in the Appendix.*

# Giving Strokes to Get Results

Dr. Eric Berne, the creator of the Transactional Analysis system of social psychology, called every form of attention a *stroke*. Maybe you have said that a person needs a lot of stroking, or compliments, and not even realized you were using a term from Transactional Analysis.

## *The Need for Attention*

When training participants are asked what would most likely result in their getting attention where they work, they almost always answer, "Messing up!" Indeed, most organizations and managers respond to mistakes and problem behavior with punitive attention. They obviously do not understand one of the most powerful truths about human behavior:

***What You Stroke Is What You Get!***

Have you ever wondered why some people make the same mistakes over and over? Why some people say and do such outlandish things? Because the need for attention is such a powerful human need, some people will do almost anything to get it. Engaging in negative behavior may be the way they learned to get attention early in their lives. If their need for attention is not being met in other ways, they will continue to stick with the one source they do have.

It doesn't make logical sense for someone to engage in behavior that results in negative responses from others. But the need for attention is emotional, not logical. What we learned as children about getting attention were powerful lessons because they met emotional needs. An emotional need often will not produce a logical behavior choice.

## *Stroking in the Workplace*

"What you stroke is what you get" applies in the workplace as in the rest of life. Whatever you give attention to, you will get more of, as in the following examples:

- ➤ If you give attention to mistakes while ignoring good work, you will have to deal with more and more mistakes
- ➤ If you give attention to late arrivals, you will have a continuing tardiness problem.
- ➤ If you give attention to meeting goals and being accountable, you will have a team that works hard to accomplish its goals and to be accountable for its actions and decisions

Many supervisors and managers struggle with putting this strategy into effect. Often that's because they have a limited repertoire of strokes. If the only strokes given are compliments and praise, the attention quickly begins to sound insincere, and the manager struggles to find new ways to reinforce the wanted behavior. Time to get creative and figure out more ways to give recognition to employees.

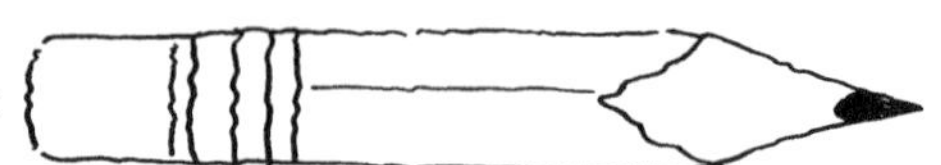

## DIFFERENT STROKES FOR DIFFERENT FOLKS

Expand your stroking repertoire. In the spaces below, list 20 ways you can give attention to employees for just being part of your team, for doing their work, for meeting their goals, for accepting responsibility, and for being accountable for the results. The first two spaces are already filled in, so you have to think of only 18 more.

| | |
|---|---|
| 1. Praise | 11. ______________ |
| 2. Compliments | 12. ______________ |
| 3. ______________ | 13. ______________ |
| 4. ______________ | 14. ______________ |
| 5. ______________ | 15. ______________ |
| 6. ______________ | 16. ______________ |
| 7. ______________ | 17. ______________ |
| 8. ______________ | 18. ______________ |
| 9. ______________ | 19. ______________ |
| 10. ______________ | 20. ______________ |

If you were unable to come up with enough forms of attention, ask others for their suggestions. How about these strokes: delegating more responsibility, asking for ideas, and listening to people. The more recognition methods you have available, the more likely you will follow through and use positive reinforcement with your employees. One of the best ways to get good performance, creativity and innovation, teamwork, and accountability for decisions and actions is to give recognition for those outcomes. It sounds simple but it takes a dedicated leader to really do it. You will be delighted with the results.

*For more ideas on employee recognition, read* Retaining Your Employees *by Barb Wingfield and Janice Berry, Crisp Publications.*

# A Recognition Certificate

Here is another idea for giving positive recognition for desirable behavior in the workplace. The certificate appeals to the "little kid" inside us and is a powerful recognition that recipients usually post in their work area. People love getting these and they display them with pride. Supply them to everyone in the organization and encourage people to hand them out whenever they see someone doing something desirable. When you get people looking for positives, guess what they find? Right! You see what you expect to see. And when you give attention for it, you will see it again and again.

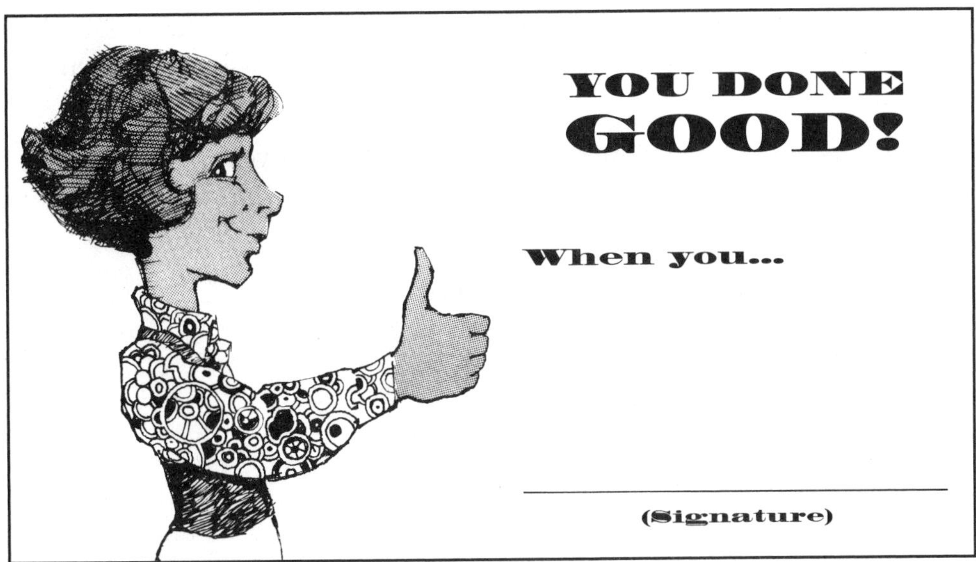

# Confronting Unacceptable Behavior

The skills you have learned so far will help you build better relationships with your team and will lead to better accountability. Still, someone on your team may continue unacceptable behavior serious enough to warrant corrective action. A final communication tool for fostering maximum accountability is that of confronting unacceptable behavior assertively. How you handle such a situation is critical to your effectiveness and your goal of encouraging accountability.

How do you respond to the word *confrontation*?

____________________________________________________________

____________________________________________________________

For most people the word conjures images of unpleasant, angry, combative sessions in which the participants are accusatory, judgmental, defensive, and uncooperative with one another. Few people have positive associations with confrontation.

Does confrontation have to be this way? Certainly not. Give it a little thought and list potential positive aspects of one person's confronting another's problem behavior.

____________________________________________________________

____________________________________________________________

## *The Positive Side of Confrontation*

As you have realized, confrontation can benefit all concerned. If someone's behavior is creating a problem for others, that person may be completely unaware of it if no one is willing to say anything. The result of saying nothing can be that the behavior continues and possibly damages relationships. This lack of awareness can explain why the "ignore the undesirable and reinforce the desirable" strategy may have failed at changing the behavior.

As an example, let's say Lee is doing something that creates a problem for you. If you take the courageous step of confronting Lee's behavior, then Lee will know that the behavior is causing difficulty and she can work on changing the behavior. Lee may very well appreciate your taking this initiative and giving her the opportunity to make a change that will preserve her relationships. If you handle the discussion skillfully, you will have resolved the problem and earned new respect from Lee in the process.

## *Caring Confrontation Formula*

The key to ensuring that confrontation produces positive outcomes is handling the confrontation skillfully. Most people don't know how to do that because they have received no training and they have no good role models from which to learn the skills. A caring confrontation involves four steps:

**STEP 1: Identify the Behavior**

**STEP 2: Identify the Tangible Effects**

**STEP 3: Identify Your Own Feelings**

**STEP 4: Identify the Change You Desire**

An exact formula cannot be devised for every situation. But when you are looking to produce a positive outcome and benefit all concerned, you should work through these four steps. With effort and practice this caring approach to confrontation will become automatic.

## 1 Identify the behavior.

Think of someone with whom you have had unsatisfactory encounters and describe the problem you have had.

____________________________________________________________

____________________________________________________________

____________________________________________________________

____________________________________________________________

Did you describe the situation in relation to the other person's characteristics? Did you use adjectives such as arrogant, lazy, passive, stupid, and uncooperative? If so, you did what most people do. Typically, when we have difficulty dealing with another person, we consider the person to be the problem.

If we define the person as the problem, we are likely to set out to change the other person in some way to resolve the difficulty. But we cannot change other people's personalities. We cannot change their core values or their lifelong attitudes. Where we are most likely to succeed is in influencing a person to change behavior.

The behavior is where the problem lies. It is what the person does that we wish they did not do, or it is what the person doesn't do that we wish they would do. It is the doing or not doing-the behavior.

You must identify the specific behavior and describe it to the other person in factual, non-blaming language. Give it a try by thinking about the same situation and person as above and describe the specific behavior(s) rather than the person. (If you did that the first time, congratulations!)

____________________________________________________________

____________________________________________________________

____________________________________________________________

____________________________________________________________

## 2 Identify the tangible effects.

Why is the other person's behavior a problem for you? Because the behavior results in or could result in an undesirable impact upon you. How does the behavior affect you? Does it cost money that comes from your budget? Does it take time and effort away from other activities? Does it affect the quality of the product you produce or the service you provide? Does it distract others from being productive? Does it contribute to a morale problem that could have a negative effect upon productivity for which you will be held accountable? List actual or possible results of the other person's behavior, making sure to list only concrete, tangible, measurable effects.

____________________________________________

____________________________________________

____________________________________________

____________________________________________

More than one or two tangible effects often result from another person's unacceptable behavior. It is these concrete results that make the behavior unacceptable.

If you can think of no concrete, tangible effects of the other person's behavior, then you probably disapprove of the behavior just because it is different from what you consider to be appropriate. You are judging the behavior by your own standards, which is a normal human tendency, but it gives you much less reason for asking someone to change his behavior. People don't like others to impose their beliefs and standards upon them, and they usually will refuse to comply (ever hear of teenager rebellion?).

When you can explain to someone how her behavior causes a tangible, negative impact upon you, then she is much more likely to change it. The tangible effect provides a rationale and helps keep you from coming across as an overbearing parent figure.

## 3 Identify your own feelings.

Whenever someone's behavior creates a problem, you are likely to respond emotionally. It is important to be aware of your feelings and to communicate them to the other person.

Many people find this aspect of confrontation challenging because few people learn much about the emotional part of being human. Many people are unaccustomed to identifying their own feelings.

You may get a better feel for your emotional responses if you realize there are only four basic human emotions-Mad, Sad, Glad, and Scared. All the other words we use to describe feelings are simply degrees of intensity of one of these four, or combinations of two or more of these basic emotions. The list below may help you recognize your own feelings whenever you experience an emotional response.

| **MAD** | **SAD** | **GLAD** | **SCARED** |
|---|---|---|---|
| irritated | unhappy | pleased | concerned |
| angry | disappointed | happy | anxious |
| annoyed | hurt | excited | threatened |
| ticked off | let down | satisfied | worried |
| disgruntled | deflated | pumped | uncertain |
| furious | lonely | exhilarated | afraid |

### Combinations

frustrated (sad+mad+scared or at least two of the three)

guilty

embarrassed

confused

jealous

suspicious

Think again about the problem situation and identify the emotions involved. You may have a different feeling tied to each tangible effect you identified in step 2.

___

___

___

By this point you may already be feeling better about the situation because you understand more about what is going on. Is this true for you?

### Identify the change you desire.

The final step is thinking about what kind of change you want. Do you simply want the person to stop using the behavior? Do you want a different behavior in place of the unacceptable one? Do you want the other person to suggest a solution?

The last question above is important. People are most likely to follow through and implement a change they thought of themselves. If you allow the other person to suggest a solution after you have presented the problem to her, you may discover that she proposes an acceptable idea. This is the ideal. She has a sense of ownership in the solution and is most likely to feel comfortable, with a sense of accomplishment, when she makes the change.

It is certainly okay for you to ask for a specific change in behavior. But giving the other person the chance to think of the change first may produce an even better result. Then if the person doesn't come up with an acceptable solution, you can offer your alternative and ask her to accept it.

Remember your rapport skills and converse with the other person in her communication style. By matching her personality type and mirroring her non-verbal signals, you can help her be more comfortable with you and the situation and to hear you most effectively. Remember to match only the assertive elements of her style.

As a rule of thumb, avoid using commands in a confrontation situation. Even Directing/Guiding personalities may rebel against your telling them what to do when you are discussing their behavior and the reasons you want it changed. Most people will react more cooperatively when you ask them to change a behavior or ask for their ideas.

## Case Study: Antagonizing Co-Workers

Randy was a good salesperson who consistently exceeded quotas and who was well liked by customers. In dealing with other employees, however, Randy often would become demanding and accusatory when others did not quite meet expectations or produce the desired results. The manager, A.J., had heard complaints about Randy's treatment of fellow employees but had never observed it himself so had chosen to say nothing to Randy.

While walking through the warehouse one day, A.J. saw Randy throw some papers onto the desk of the shipping supervisor, Sean, and heard Randy yelling at Sean, "When are you idiots going to learn that 'Special Handling - Rush' means to get the blasted shipment to the customer as fast as possible? If you keep screwing up my special orders, I'm going to lose important customers, which means the company loses money, which may mean you lose your job!"

A.J. walked away and decided this event provided the evidence needed for a confrontation with Randy. After taking a little time to prepare, A.J. asked Randy for a convenient appointment and told Randy they would meet in the conference room where they would not be disturbed.

A.J. greeted Randy in the conference room and said, "Randy, I've been concerned for some time about reports I've heard, and I was in the warehouse this morning when I witnessed your shouting at Sean and throwing some papers on his desk. I was disappointed about what I saw and heard, which is why I wanted to talk with you."

Randy responded with a flushed face and in a rapid delivery, "I was only trying to get Sean to understand that customer service is important. Those shipping people are constantly messing up special orders and they just don't seem to understand how that undermines all of my hard work!"

A.J. responded, "Randy, I know you are concerned about providing good service for your customers, and I'm concerned about that, too. That is why I need you to understand another concern of mine. Are you willing to hear it?" Randy looked at A.J. somewhat skeptically but said, "Okay. Shoot!"

A.J. continued, "My big concern is that if you treat Sean and others here with the disrespect I witnessed this morning, you will actually receive less cooperation from them rather than more, and your customers will receive worse service, not better. I suspect that is not what you want. True?" Randy quickly responded, "Of course I don't want that!"

A.J. then asked, "Randy, will you promise me that you will use your excellent selling skills with your co-workers just like you do with your customers and sell them on the importance of making special efforts on your special orders?" To which Randy responded, "Sure. I can do that. You're right, A.J. I don't want them to sabotage my orders. Thanks for saying something. I guess I wasn't using my head, was I?" A.J. laughed and said, "Randy, I couldn't have said it better. I know you have the brains and the skills for handling situations to get the best results and I'm glad to hear that you're willing to do it. Thanks!"

---

Was Randy asked to admit to being wrong? ❑ Yes ❑ No

Was Randy lectured about not using his skills? ❑ Yes ❑ No

How did A.J. describe Randy's behavior?

______________________________________________

______________________________________________

What was the tangible effect of Randy's behavior that A.J. mentioned?

______________________________________________

______________________________________________

What was the emotion that A.J. described?

______________________________________________

______________________________________________

What was the behavior change to which Randy agreed?

______________________________________________

______________________________________________

*Compare your responses to the author's suggestions in the Appendix.*

## *Confrontation Made Easy*

Are you thinking, "Yeah, but most problems can't be resolved that easily"? Many people have doubts about being able to resolve problem behaviors easily and are sometimes surprised when people turn out to be more cooperative than anticipated. Certainly, some situations may be more complex than this one, and people can be much more defensive when confronted. Even then, the situation can be resolved with a win-win outcome by using the skills explained in this book.

Did you notice how A.J. used active listening when responding to Randy's defensive reaction to being confronted? Rather than allowing the defensive retort to sidetrack the discussion, A.J. restated it and used it as a springboard to explaining that the same concern for customer service is what prompted the whole discussion. This meant that Randy's own concern was now being used as an incentive to get Randy to change his behavior, which is why it turned out to be so easy. If A.J. were not a skilled listener, that opportunity probably would have been missed and the discussion might have taken much longer and might not have had such a successful conclusion.

Randy seemed to be aware that he was accountable for customer satisfaction as well as sales, and it was much more effective for A.J. to use that sense of accountability in the positive manner above than it would have been to blame or criticize.

Even excellent techniques require skillful use, which is why you are encouraged to practice frequently and consistently after reading this book. Just understanding the concepts and tools is not enough to improve your effectiveness.

## Confronting Your Co-worker

Using the person and situation you have been examining through the caring confrontation formula, write below what you would say to begin the discussion. Remember, you do not have to use all of the pieces in your opening statement just as A.J. used only a couple items to get started. Remember to match the communication style of the other person in your word choices and delivery.

**Your opening statement:**

______________________________________________________________________

______________________________________________________________________

______________________________________________________________________

______________________________________________________________________

______________________________________________________________________

Ask someone to read what you have written and ask how it sounds. Is it non-blaming? Is it factual rather than judgmental? Do the words invite the other person to feel respected? It is sometimes hard to evaluate our own word choices, so having someone else provide feedback can help improve what you will say.

**What kind of defensive response might the other person use in reaction to your opening statement?**

______________________________________________________________________

______________________________________________________________________

______________________________________________________________________

______________________________________________________________________

**If the other person does say that, how will you respond using active listening feedback?**

______________________________________________________________________

______________________________________________________________________

______________________________________________________________________

______________________________________________________________________

## *Engage in Active Listening*

Be prepared to use active listening feedback several times if the person continues being defensive and emotional in reaction to your confrontation. People are not accustomed to direct confrontation. People tend to get others to back off and leave them alone by being defensive, so you will need to be prepared to use your skills to invite them to become less emotional and defensive.

Only when the person is calmer will you be able to continue working toward a commitment for change. You must continue the discussion until you receive that commitment. It is okay to call a timeout to allow you both to recover your poise, but then resume the discussion and get the commitment for change. Without this commitment, you have not accomplished your goal.

Do you see how this approach encourages people to be accountable for their own behavior and its consequences? By treating people as responsible adults, you are telling them that you expect them to honor their commitments and to be responsible for their choices. If you treat people like misbehaving children, how do you think they will behave? That communicates very different expectations and produces predictably different results.

# Performing a Relationship Audit

As you have learned, building maximum accountability comes from developing open, trusting relationships. But problems often persist in relationships because we avoid the potentially unpleasant task of examining how well the relationship is working. It is easier to overlook some problems and hope that everything will work out in the end. Unfortunately, denial only allows problems to continue, feelings to fester, and individuals to avoid being accountable for their role in whatever difficulties exist in the relationship.

In the workplace people are accustomed to performance reviews every six months or year. But the relationship audit is different. It is an opportunity for you and your employee to give each other feedback, not about performance, but about the workings of the relationship itself. Using the relationship audit and other techniques in this book will help you improve the relationship and improve the effectiveness of your performance reviews.

For this audit to be effective, each person must have learned about and developed the skills covered in this book and its companion, *Self-Empowerment**. Without these, the relationship audit will be difficult to complete successfully because it involves each person being direct and honest with the other while communicating about significant relationship factors

---

* *Sam R. Lloyd and Tina Berthelot,* Self-Empowerment, *Crisp Publications.*

# THE RELATIONSHIP AUDIT WORKSHEET

1. List below your understanding of the basic reasons for the relationship. Consider the relationship's goals, commitments, and potential benefits. Think about any unstated expectations or "rules" that may have developed.

______________________________

______________________________

______________________________

______________________________

2. What wants and needs of yours are satisfied in this relationship?

______________________________

______________________________

3. Which wants and needs would you like to have better satisfied in this relationship?

______________________________

______________________________

4. What does the other person do well in this relationship? (Consider such things as expressing wants and needs, providing information, communicating expectations and feelings, giving feedback, making decisions, problem solving, and listening.)

______________________________

______________________________

5. What can the other person improve upon?

______________________________

______________________________

6. What do you do well in this relationship?

______________________________

______________________________

7. What can you do better?

_______________________________________________

_______________________________________________

8. What suggestions do you have for improving this relationship?

_______________________________________________

_______________________________________________

_______________________________________________

_______________________________________________

Which of the items on the worksheet were most difficult for you to answer? (Check (✔) all that apply.)

❑ 1 ❑ 2 ❑ 3 ❑ 4 ❑ 5 ❑ 6 ❑ 7 ❑ 8

For each item checked, explain briefly why it was difficult.

_______________________________________________

_______________________________________________

_______________________________________________

_______________________________________________

For each item checked, think of at least one idea for helping you do it more easily.

_______________________________________________

_______________________________________________

_______________________________________________

_______________________________________________

*This worksheet may be photocopied for individual use.*

## *Discussing the Relationship Audit*

After each person completes the worksheet, agree upon a time and place to share your results and provide feedback for each other. This feedback can trigger strong emotions, so you must agree in advance about how to handle the discussion and be prepared to use your communication skills.

Begin the discussion by talking about the audit's purpose, which is to work together to improve the relationship for the benefit of all concerned. To help you both become more comfortable giving and receiving feedback:

- Practice exchanging the information orally rather than just reading each other's papers
- Give your feedback accurately, respectfully, and sensitively to help each other hear what the other has to say
- Agree in advance to listen without interrupting while the other is sharing the results of his preparation
- Respond with active listening restatements when you do speak
- Avoid explaining yourself, denying the accuracy of the other's feedback, countering with your own feedback (you will get your turn), apologizing, or anything other than acknowledging what you hear

The potential for developing an even better relationship from this audit is great, which should be an incentive for each person to be open, honest, receptive, and cooperative. The audit is designed to produce a win-win outcome in which each person gets his needs met, but only you and the other(s) can assure that outcome.

## *A Sample Relationship Audit Discussion*

This is an abbreviated example of how the audit discussion unfolds when each person uses the concepts and skills from this book. A manager and an employee are using their worksheets and have agreed to take turns with each item rather than having one person go through the entire worksheet first.

**Employee:** *"I see our relationship being one in which we share responsibility for defining short-term and long-term goals for our work, but in which you have the final say because you are my boss. Our relationship exists for the purpose of designing and manufacturing our company's products and providing each of us with income and personal accomplishments."*

**Manager:** *"I hear that you view our relationship as being one with shared responsibility but with my having more power because of my position. True?"*

**Employee:** *"Yes. That's accurate. How do you see it?"*

**Manager:** *"I wrote something very similar. Our relationship is for the purpose of accomplishing the work we have agreed to do for the company, and we do it by working together to define our goals and complete the tasks necessary to accomplish them. I believe we do it by consensus in which everyone has an equal say in determining what we do and how we do it, so I was surprised to hear you say that I have the final say."*

**Employee:** *"It sounds like we have a similar perception of our relationship, and I agree that we do use the consensus approach very well most of the time. I guess my comment was a way of acknowledging your higher level of authority and responsibility, and that there are times when you have to make some decisions and ask us to support you. That's true, isn't it?"*

**Manager:** *"Hmmm. Yes, I guess that's right. Is that a problem for you?"*

**Employee:** *"No. It's unrealistic to try to make every decision a consensus. It takes too much time."*

## Comments about the Sample Discussion

Do you perceive now how this kind of discussion can be carried out? When each person uses listening skills and communicates assertively, the discussion can be productive and satisfying.

If emotions erupt, using active listening feedback will help lower the emotional level so the content is heard correctly and each person's feelings, wants, and needs are acknowledged and respected.

## *The Discussion Continues*

Skipping to a later point in the discussion, the two people are giving feedback to each other about item 5 on the checklist (what the other person can do better).

**Employee:** *"Oh boy! This is the hard part-having to tell you how to improve!"*

**Manager:** *"Yeah, I know. I've never liked giving people negative feedback, but it's important so let's do our best. I think we can both do a little growing here."*

**Employee:** *"Okay. One of the things I wrote is that you have room for improvement in your facilitation skills in our meetings. A lot of our meetings take longer than necessary because you seem to have a problem maintaining control over the discussion and allow a couple of people to get us off track on their favorite subjects."*

**Manager:** *"You're saying that I need to learn more about how to get people to stick to the agenda and not allow them to sidetrack discussion onto topics they like to discuss that are not relevant. Right?"*

**Employee:** *"Exactly. Fred and Joan always want to talk about their pet peeves, which we all have heard before and you sometimes let them get away with it for 15-20 minutes. It not only wastes our time but it also usually changes the whole tone of the meeting, and it takes us longer to get everybody back into being positive and creative again."*

**Manager:** *"Yeah. Now that you mention it, I have noticed in some of our discussions that the whole mood shifts suddenly and we seem to lose our momentum. I just hadn't put together that it was happening because of someone pulling us off on a tangent. That's a very helpful insight!"*

### Additional Comments

This sample demonstrates how valuable a relationship audit can be. Often the participants in such a discussion will learn valuable insights from one another, which can help to improve their relationship and their effectiveness.

You probably noticed how tactfully but directly the employee worded the feedback, which helped the manager hear it without feeling attacked. Did you also notice that the manager's immediate response was to restate the feedback using the active listening restatement technique? Doing this benefits both people–the employee knows immediately that the feedback has been heard and understood correctly, and the manager is better able to understand the feedback and feel okay about it without becoming defensive.

## How Will You Say It?

Practice the challenging component of telling the other person what she can do better in the relationship. Refer to your audit worksheet and read what you wrote in item 5. Write below how you will say this to the other person using factual, non-blaming language. Remember to avoid exaggeration, judgment, and words and phrases that tend to trigger emotional responses in the other person.

______________________________________________

______________________________________________

______________________________________________

______________________________________________

______________________________________________

______________________________________________

You may have an intuitive awareness of what the other person might tell you to do better in the relationship. Assume that the person has just given you this feedback and did not do it very skillfully. Practice writing an active listening response to this less-than-skillful feedback

______________________________________________

______________________________________________

______________________________________________

______________________________________________

Knowing how to say assertively what you want others to hear, how to match their personality type for better rapport, and how to use active listening feedback to confirm understanding and demonstrate empathy can create a valuable sense of personal power and control for anyone. Completing a relationship audit periodically can make a powerful difference in the level of trust and mutual respect in the relationship, which helps to assure maximum accountability from each person involved.

*P A R T* **5**

# Follow-Up Ideas for Skill Development

# Maintain Your Momentum

If you want to ensure that your investment of time and money will pay the dividends you desire, commit yourself to do follow-up work. This part suggests ways to help you maintain your momentum and put into practice the techniques and skills you have learned.

We know from research in adult learning that within 24 hours you will start forgetting as much as 70% of what you learned. Even if you agree that the ideas, techniques, and skills presented in this book make sense and can help you improve your effectiveness-and even if you have completed all of the exercises while reading the book-if you now put the book aside and do nothing else, you will probably discover that you quickly return to old behavior patterns.

Here are suggestions to help you counteract this high rate of forgetting and lodge the material more firmly in your long-term memory:

- Within 24 hours, review the book and your work in the exercises
- Review it all again after another week
- Explain to someone else what you learned and how you will use what you learned
- Set goals for yourself to help ensure that you follow through and put into action those ideas and techniques that appeal to you

# Establish an Action Plan

As you learned in Part 3, the road to accomplishment starts with clearly defined goals. Write down your own goals and action steps for following up on what you have learned in this book. Remember to make your goal statements meet the SMARTS criteria.

**Follow-up Goal 1:**

______________________________

______________________________

**Action Steps to Accomplish This Goal:**

______________________________

______________________________

______________________________

**Follow-up Goal 2:**

______________________________

______________________________

**Action Steps to Accomplish This Goal:**

______________________________

______________________________

______________________________

**Follow-up Goal 3:**

______________________________

______________________________

**Action Steps to Accomplish This Goal:**

______________________________

______________________________

______________________________

______________________________

# Reward Yourself

When you do carry out your plans, practice the techniques and skills you've learned, and make changes in how you handle yourself in the situations you encounter, reward yourself. As you have learned in this book, behavior that gets attention is reinforced.

You will likely receive positive attention from others when you use the skills and handle interactions with others more effectively. But you can make sure to reinforce your new behaviors by planning your own rewards for yourself.

Rewarding the "little kid" who lives within your personality is particularly effective. This is the part of you that is emotional, intuitive, creative, spontaneous, and playful. This is the part in each of us that is most responsive to attention.

## What Does Your "Little Kid" Like?

Check (✔) all of the following that appeal to the young child inside you. Be spontaneous and playful as you read the list. (And turn off that disapproving parent who lives inside you.)

- ❑ **Having a party**
- ❑ **New clothes**
- ❑ **Surprises**
- ❑ **"Fun food" treats**
- ❑ **Spectator sports**
- ❑ **Dancing**
- ❑ **Travel**
- ❑ **Books, new software**
- ❑ **Gifts**
- ❑ **Playing sports**
- ❑ **Recorded music**
- ❑ **Going to movies/theater**
- ❑ **Making love**
- ❑ **Comedy**
- ❑ **Night out with boys/girls**
- ❑ **Praise, applause**

Did you find some that appeal to you? When you are in the mood to let yourself have what your heart desires, list other rewards that would motivate you to follow through and accomplish your goals. List anything you want.

**More fun stuff I like:**

________________________________________

________________________________________

________________________________________

________________________________________

________________________________________

________________________________________

Now that you have identified rewards you would enjoy, make definite plans to give one or more of these to yourself when you complete an action step or when you achieve a goal within a set time limit. Ask someone to give you one of these rewards when they see you doing what you have committed to. Or have them surprise you with a reward if they notice your becoming discouraged. What a wonderful way to involve others in your personal development program. The idea works and it will help you achieve your goals.

# Continue to Work at It

Slipping back into old behavior patterns is all too easy to do. The following are a few more ways to help you stick with your commitment to follow through, use the ideas and techniques, and practice the skills:

- **Read more books**. A list of recommended books is on page 110, and you can find others in your favorite bookstore or library or on the Internet. Reading related materials will reinforce the concepts learned in this book.

- **Get training.** Participating in training that covers these ideas and skills will enable you to reinforce what you learned and to practice techniques and skills. Check what is available through your organization's training and development program, from universities, and from public-seminar firms. An Internet search also will help you identify training programs that could help you continue your development. Be sure to check www.trainingforsuccess.com.

- **Practice! Practice! Practice!** Understanding is not enough to change your behavior. To develop any skill with new techniques and behaviors, you must practice them repeatedly.

- **Keep a journal.** Writing about how you used something from this book will help you remember to follow through and put it into practice. Even if you were not successful in a particular situation, take a few minutes to think about it, write about it in your journal, and decide how you could do better next time.

These steps will help you learn from your practice and stay with the goal of using what you learned from working through this book.

# *A P P E N D I X*

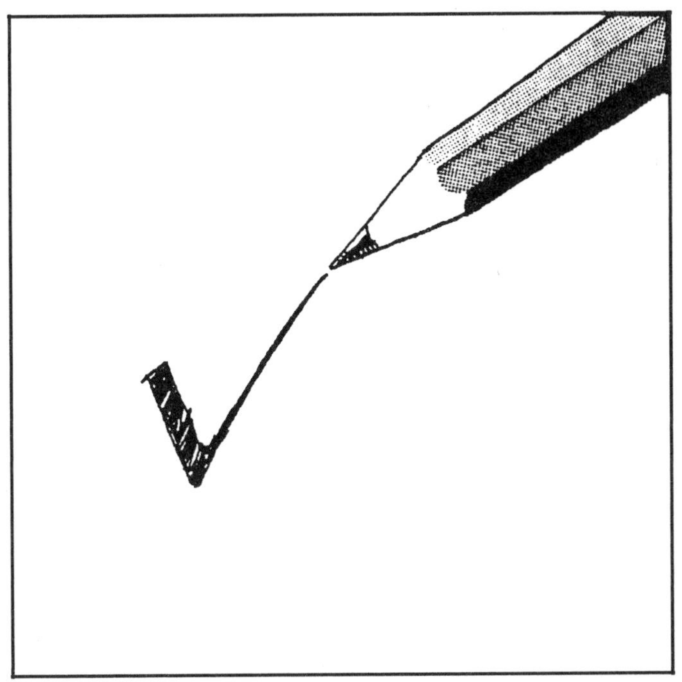

# Author's Notes on the Case Studies

## Sharing the Workload (page 4)

If you checked all but number 1, you agree with the author. We cannot know how the employee felt about the assignments, but we can recognize the mistakes made in the delegation. No clear agreement existed about what was expected of the employee, when the work was due, or the work's importance. In this case, most of the problem's responsibility rests with the manager, but the employee could have helped prevent the problems by asking questions, so each of them contributed to the unsatisfactory outcome.

So, who is accountable in this unfortunate scenario? The manager blamed the employee for being irresponsible, but the manager's boss did not agree. The manager received a stern lecture about being accountable for the results even if the work was delegated to others.

A tough aspect of accountability is that it cannot be delegated. You can delegate responsibility for results, and you can delegate authority (power) to produce the results, but you can't pass off the ultimate accountability, which was originally assigned to you.

The manager could have used the situation to demonstrate confidence in the employee and to communicate the importance of the work being assigned and the rewards that would result from successful outcomes (credit, extra time off, a celebratory dinner). This might have made the employee more likely to be accountable for his work, which would have helped his manager fulfill her responsibility.

The employee also would have been more likely to recognize this as an opportunity to strengthen his relationship with the manager and to juggle his priorities to get the assignment completed well and on time (if the discussion had included information about timelines).

The goal of this book is to help you prevent such problems with your own employees and build relationships to support maximum accountability. Accountability is not a problem when relationships are built on trust, mutual respect, clear communication, clearly negotiated agreements, skillful delegation, reinforcement of desired behaviors, and appropriate handling of problems and mistakes.

## A Negative Self-Fulfilling Prophecy (page 11)

Possibly the message Pat received was to submit only ideas that have been thoroughly researched and prepared in a formal proposal. More likely: Do not bother coming up with improvement ideas. "Just do your job and don't think."

Messages such as these could discourage even a highly motivated person. Pat could just give up and stop suggesting ideas or might even go to another organization where new ideas were welcomed. Even people with high self-esteem can begin to doubt themselves when their manager consistently communicates negative expectations.

In most cases such as this, the manager is not intentionally discouraging the employee. The messages often result from the manager's perception that employees don't know as much about running the business as managers do or that improvement is the manager's responsibility. Casey probably did not even realize what was being communicated to Pat.

In most relationships the self-fulfilling prophecy messages are even more subtle. In controlled research projects in which false information was given to teachers about certain students, the expectations created by the false information were communicated over a period of weeks and months. The expectations became reality, even though they were based on false information. Videotapes showed that communications as subtle as frequency of eye contact, touch, smiles, or greetings–or the lack of these communications-day after day produced the expected results.

The point is that your expectations of others do get communicated even though you may believe that you are keeping them secret. What do you think about others?

## A Positive Self-Fulfillling Prophecy (page 14)

In this case the manager decided that the employee was capable of doing more and communicated those expectations consistently. This communication helped Peter decide that he was indeed capable of achieving this new goal that he had not previously considered.

Are you willing to make a little extra effort to help your employees develop new skills and improve upon existing ones? You will gain as much as they if you choose to follow this executive's example and put self-fulfilling prophecy to work for positive outcomes.

## Delegating or Dumping? (page 40)

Marvin's instructions are specific and clear, but he could improve on all other counts. Marvin is guilty of a common management mistake. He doesn't seem to understand the difference between delegating and dumping. By assigning specific and somewhat menial tasks to Tony each month, he is ignoring the opportunity to redesign the whole reporting system, which could provide a one-time solution for his problem. He has dumped a boring, routine task on an employee when he could have delegated a challenging responsibility.

Marvin repeats his mistake with Ellen by dumping the undesirable task of lecturing the support staff rather than investigating the problem to discover the root causes. Ellen attempts to suggest that other aspects need to be considered, but she is interrupted by her manager, who apparently assumes that his answers are the only right ones.

You can imagine the conversation between Tony and Ellen after they leave Marvin's office. Do you think their respect for their manager might have dropped a notch or two? How do you think they feel about their assignments?

## Delegating to Empower (page 46)

Quite an improvement, right? This is still not a perfect delegation, but excellence does not require perfection. With this approach, Tony and Marvin will have a better relationship. Tony will do a better job with this assignment, and the improvement in efficiency will be many times greater than the original approach. Tony has willingly and enthusiastically accepted this responsibility and knows he is accountable for the results. Marvin also has grown a little in his self-empowerment by having empowered Tony.

Like any other skill, delegation is developed with practice. Knowing what to do is not enough by itself.*

**For more help with improving your delegation skills, see* Delegating for Results *by Robert Maddux, Crisp Publications.*

## One Mistake Leads to Another (page 49)

If you said his mistakes included failing to follow up the delegation in writing or failing to make sure the follow-up was carried out as agreed (remember the weekly progress report?), you are right. If you said another mistake was confronting Tony in front of his peers, you agree with the author. An important element in handling the mistakes of others is choosing an appropriate time and place.

## A Positive Learning Experience (pages 53)

Obviously, this approach takes a few more minutes than scolding Tony in the hallway, but the outcome is well worth the extra time and effort. Tony has gained respect for Marvin because he handled the situation so skillfully and because he revealed a little of his own imperfections. Tony also will have less fear about accepting new responsibilities and being accountable for his decisions and actions when he knows his boss will handle mistakes in this positive coaching manner. Marvin has added to his own success by turning a problem into an improvement in his relationship with Tony, and Tony's project is more likely to conclude successfully.*

## Accountability through Communication (pages 66–67)

When you do a side-by-side comparison like this, the differences in behavior styles become obvious and the results of the behavior are predictable. Did you predict that Kelly's employees would be comfortable being accountable to her? You may also have guessed that these employees would gladly accept delegated responsibility and are probably accustomed to being trusted with responsibility. The team probably would take the initiative to do their best for this manager. Kelly's behavior style was assertive.

---

**For additional ideas on improving your coaching skills as part of your self-empowerment growth, read* Coaching and Counseling *by Marianne Minor, Crisp Publications.*

Terry's behavior style, on the other hand, was nonassertive. His body language and words communicated a lack of comfort and a considerable amount of uncertainty. When the indirect request for ideas failed to prompt a response other than silence, Terry jumped in to fill the uncomfortable silence with words that communicated he had already abandoned the whole idea. He did not say whether the meeting was adjourned, and one of the employees had to ask if it was.

It is highly unlikely that Terry's employees would have confidence in his leadership or trust that he would serve as their champion when needed. You probably guessed that they also would be uncomfortable being accountable for their decisions, actions, and mistakes with such a nonassertive manager. To be comfortable they would need to know their manager would be assertive enough to stand up for them when things didn't go smoothly. You might also have guessed that the employees probably do as they please most of the time, knowing that Terry is unlikely to question what they do or confront unacceptable behavior.

You might have guessed that Morgan's employees also would be uncomfortable with accountability and afraid to take chances or make mistakes, but for a different reason: Morgan's behavior style was aggressive. The message was clear–the manager didn't really expect the team to come up with any good ideas. The other message communicated was that the manager was superior to the employees. These employees are unlikely to take much initiative for fear of displeasing their manager. Instead, they simply wait to do what they are told.

Remember self-fulfilling prophecy? These are examples of how communication produces self-fulfilling outcomes. Terry's lack of confidence will repeatedly result in a lack of cooperation, loss of respect, and poor leadership. Morgan's act of superiority and disrespectful messages will produce a submissive, passive team with some employees retaliating with passive-aggressive behavior, such as arriving late, forgetting duties, and taking long breaks. Kelly's assertive behavior will result in loyal employees who take pride in their work and accomplishments. Day after day messages are delivered through the managers' behavior.*

---

**To learn more about becoming more assertive, read* Developing Positive Assertiveness *by Sam R. Lloyd, Crisp Publications.*

## Antagonizing Co-Workers (pages 78-79)

Randy was not asked to admit to being wrong.

Randy was not lectured.

The behavior description was "shouting at Sean and throwing some papers on his desk."

The tangible effect was "less cooperation from them rather than more and your customers will receive worse service, not better."

Randy agreed to use good selling skills with the co-workers.

# Author's Suggested Responses to Exercises

## Recognizing Rapport (page 16)

Items 1, 2, 4, 5, 6, and 9 are typical indicators of rapport. For further explanation about the answers, continue reading.

Items 3 and 10 might be evidence of rapport but not necessarily. Each person can be angry with the other or expressing concern, frustration or anxiety and still have rapport and be communicating successfully. Some people operate at a faster pace than others, but when all participants in the communication are fast paced they can have excellent rapport. What is important is that they are at about the same emotional level and understanding each other. That is why 7 and 8 were not selected as evidence of rapport. People can be swearing and talking loudly yet have good rapport with each other; they are talking the same language and are "in synch" with each other.

## Practice Empathic Responses (page 24)

Remember, the content can be paraphrased in many ways. Often several possible emotions could be present for you to acknowledge.

*"You sound really frustrated about trying to work with Pat, and you're telling me that you waste a lot of time arguing, right?"*

*"You seem concerned about our old stuff and you want to know when we're going to upgrade. Am I hearing you correctly?"*

*"So you're letting me know that you're checking out other opportunities because you're discouraged with advancement opportunities here. True?"*

## Name that Type (page 59)

1. Analytical - asking for more detailed information
2. Expressive - spontaneous emotional reaction
3. Directing - authoritative statement of opinion
4. Directing - commanding; my solution is the solution
5. Supporting - concern for others
6. Analytical - logical explanation, impersonal and sophisticated word choices
7. Expressive - brief, said with exclamation point, self-concerned
8. Directing - judgmental, commanding
9. Supporting - taking care of someone else
10. Analytical - postulating about a situation, using big words
11. Supporting - focused on relationships and pleasing others
12. Directing - forceful statement of opinions, judging others

## Personality Type and Pacing (page 60)

Do your examples sound something like these?

**Directing/Guiding** - "Kelly, the project deadline has changed. Please have your part of it done by the end of this month."

**Supporting/Caring** - "Kelly, I've just learned that our project deadline has changed, so we'll have to speed up a little. I'm sorry for having to put pressure on you, but will you please have your part finished by the end of this month?"

**Analytical** - "Kelly, I have just been informed that our budget analysis project deadline has been accelerated which means that we will be required to have the components completed by the end of this month. Will you please make that change on your calendar?"

**Expressive** - "Kelly! Time to throw our project into high gear! Our deadline has been moved up, so we have to have everything wrapped up by the end of this month. Deal?"

## Win, Lose, or Win-Win (page 64)

1. Assertive - a direct request for action
2. Aggressive - disrespectful and invites the other person to feel inadequate
3. Assertive - a direct command
4. Nonassertive - tentative, communicates a lack of confidence
5. Aggressive - controlling, sarcastic
6. Nonassertive - somewhat self-deprecating and hesitant
7. Nonassertive - submissive and self-deprecating
8. Assertive - honest expression of emotion followed by a request for feedback
9. Aggressive - inappropriately commanding, accusatory
10. Assertive - direct appropriate compliment
11. Nonassertive - hesitant, indirect (no direct request or command)
12. Assertive - spontaneous expression of joy and pride of achievement
13. Aggressive - belittling comment
14. Nonassertive - tentative, submissive-allowing others to choose rather than choosing for oneself
15. Aggressive - appropriate command followed by a sarcastic accusation

# Recommended Reading

Alessandra, Tony and Michael O'Connor. *People Smarts.* NY: Pfeiffer, 1994.

Bonet, Diana. *The Business of Listening, Third Edition.* Menlo Park, CA: Crisp Publications, 2001.

Braham, Barb and Janice Berry. *Retaining Your Employees.* Menlo Park, CA: Crisp Publications, 2001.

Byham, William. *Zapp! The Lightning of Empowerment.* NY: Ballantine Group, 1997.

Kouzes, James and Barry Posner. *The Leadership Challenge.* NY: Jossey-Bass, 1996.

LaBorde, Genie Z. *Influencing with Integrity.* Palo Alto, CA: Syntony, 1983.

LeBoeuf, Michael. *The Greatest Management Principle in the World.* NY: Berkley, 1985.

Lloyd, Sam R. *Developing Positive Assertiveness, Third Edition.* Menlo Park, CA: Crisp Publications, 2002.

Lloyd, Sam R. *Leading Teams: The Skills for Success.* Urbandale, IA: American Media, 1996.

Lloyd, Sam and Tina Berthelot, *Self-Empowerment, Revised Edition.* Menlo Park, CA: Crisp Publications, 2002.

Minor, Marianne. *Coaching & Counseling, Third Edition.* Menlo Park, CA: Crisp Publications, 2002.

# CRISP WORLDWIDE DISTRIBUTION

English language books are distributed worldwide. Major international distributors include:

## ASIA/PACIFIC

*Australia/New Zealand:* In Learning, PO Box 1051, Springwood QLD, Brisbane, Australia 4127 Tel: 61-7-3-841-2286, Facsimile: 61-7-3-841-1580 ATTN: Messrs. Richard/Robert Gordon

*Malaysia, Philippines, Singapore:* Epsys Pte Ltd., 540 Sims Ave #04-01, Sims Avenue Centre, 387603, Singapore Tel: 65-747-1964, Facsimile: 65-747-0162 ATTN: Mr. Jack Chin

*Hong Kong/Mainland China:* Crisp Learning Solutions, 18/F Honest Motors Building 9-11 Leighton Rd., Causeway Bay, Hong Kong Tel: 852-2915-7119, Facsimile: 852-2865-2815 ATTN: Ms. Grace Lee

*Japan:* Phoenix Associates, Believe Mita Bldg., 8th Floor 3-43-16 Shiba, Minato-ku, Tokyo 105-0014, Japan Tel: 81-3-5427-6231, Facsimile: 81-3-5427-6232 ATTN: Mr. Peter Owans

## CANADA

Crisp Learning Canada, 60 Briarwood Avenue, Mississauga, ON L5G 3N6 Canada
Tel: 905-274-5678, Facsimile: 905-278-2801
ATTN: Mr. Steve Connolly

## EUROPEAN UNION

*England:* Flex Learning Media, Ltd., 9-15 Hitchin Street,
Baldock, Hertfordshire, SG7 6AL, England
Tel: 44-1-46-289-6000, Facsimile: 44-1-46-289-2417 ATTN: Mr. David Willetts

## INDIA

Multi-Media HRD, Pvt. Ltd., National House, Floor 1
6 Tulloch Road, Appolo Bunder, Bombay, India 400-039
Tel: 91-22-204-2281, Facsimile: 91-22-283-6478
ATTN: Messrs. Ajay Aggarwal/ C.L. Aggarwal

## SOUTH AMERICA

*Mexico:* Grupo Editorial Iberoamerica, Nebraska 199, Col. Napoles, 03810 Mexico, D.F. Tel: 525-523-0994, Facsimile: 525-543-1173 ATTN: Señor Nicholas Grepe

## SOUTH AFRICA

*Bookstores*: Alternative Books, PO Box 1345, Ferndale 2160, South Africa Tel: 27-11-792-7730, Facsimile: 27-11-792-7787 ATTN: Mr. Vernon de Haas

*Corporate*: Learning Resources, P.O. Box 2806, Parklands, Johannesburg 2121, South Africa, Tel: 27-21-531-2923, Facsimile: 27-21-531-2944 ATTN: Mr. Ricky Robinson

## MIDDLE EAST

Edutech Middle East, L.L.C., PO Box 52334, Dubai U.A.E.
Tel: 971-4-359-1222, Facsimile: 971-4-359-6500 ATTN: Mr. A.S.F. Karim